long nights
and log fires

Warming comfort food for family and friends

RYLAND

PETERS

& SMALL

LONDON NEW YORK

Senior Designer Toni Kay
Senior Commissioning Editor Julia Charles
Picture Research Emily Westlake
Production Toby Marshall
Art Director Leslie Harrington
Publishing Director Alison Starling
Indexer Hilary Bird

First published in hardback in the United States
in 2009
This paperback edition published in 2011 by
Ryland Peters & Small, Inc.
519 Broadway, 5th Floor
New York, NY 10012
www.rylandpeters.com

10 9 8 7 6 5 4 3 2 1

Text © Ghillie Basan, Fiona Beckett, Susannah
Blake, Maxine Clark, Linda Collister, Ross Dobson,
Lydia France, Liz Franklin, Manisha Gambhir
Harkins, Tonia George, Kate Habershon, Caroline
Marson, Louise Pickford, Ben Reed, Fiona Smith,
Sonia Stevenson, Fran Warde, Laura Washburn,
and Ryland Peters & Small 2009, 2011

Design and photographs
© Ryland Peters & Small 2009, 2011

ISBN: 978-1-84975-154-4

The hardback edition of this book is cataloged as
follows:

Library of Congress Cataloging-in-Publication Data
Long nights and log fires : warming comfort food for
family and friends.
     p. cm.
  Includes index.
  ISBN 978-1-84597-919-5
  1. Cookery.
  TX714.L658 2009
  641.5--dc22
                        2009020732

Printed and bound in China.

Notes

• All spoon measurements are level, unless otherwise stated.
• All herbs used in the recipes in this book are fresh unless specified as dried.
• Eggs are medium unless otherwise specified. Uncooked or partially cooked eggs should not be served
to the very old, frail, young children, pregnant women, or those with compromised immune systems.
• When a recipe calls for the grated peel of lemons or limes or uses slices of fruit, buy unwaxed fruit and
wash well before using. If you can only find treated fruit, scrub well in warm soapy water before using.
• Ovens should be preheated to the specifed temperature. Recipes in this book were tested in a regular
oven. If using a fan-assisted oven, follow the manufacturer's instructions for adjusting temperatures.

long nights
and log fires

contents

come in from the cold...

Chilly days and long dark evenings were made for staying indoors and taking the time to prepare hearty, warming, and sustaining food for family and friends. When the cold wind blows and the snow piles up outside, where better to be than at the heart of a warm kitchen, enjoying the aromas of good home cooking wafting from the oven? This book is intended to be as warming as a log fire on a cold winter's night and offers a wealth of delicious recipes for comfort food and warming drinks.

What could be more welcome on a freezing cold day that a steaming hot bowl of soup? It's time to give your tired old soup-making repertoire a new lease of life—here you'll find old favorites such as Leek and Potato Soup but also some tasty and original ideas like Pumpkin Soup with Sage and Honey or Parsnip, Chorizo, and Chestnut Soup. Warm and sustaining savory snacks are a must to keep energy reserves up in the colder months. With quick and easy recipes to try from Parmesan and Bacon Pancakes with Chive Butter to Smoked Trout Rarebit, you'll never be stuck for inspiration again.

Casual dinner dishes are perfect for two people or for weekday family meals. Recipes include Herby Sausages on Polenta with Red Onion and Red Currant Jelly or Chicken, Leek, and Tarragon Pot Pie. One-pot wonders were made for cooking on winter days—from slow-cooked French classics such as Boeuf Bourguignon to exotic Moroccan tagines, once assembled these casserole-style dishes can be put in the oven and left to cook themselves.

A roast has to be everyone's idea of a delicious, homey family meal and one that many of us remember fondly from our childhoods. You can recreate that same warm ambience with the recipes included here—from Italian-style Roast Pork with White Wine, Garlic, and Fennel to the "king of roasts", Roast Fillet of Beef with Herbed Yorkshire Puddings. Roasting can bring out the best in poultry, game, and fish too. Try Roast Chicken with Bay Leaves, Thyme, and Lemon, Roasted Pheasant Breasts with Bacon, Shallots, and Mushrooms or delicious Roasted Salmon Wrapped in Prosciutto.

Interesting sides can turn a simple roast or rustic casserole into something very special. Forget dull and soggy boiled vegetables—enticing recipes here include Garlic Sautéed Green Beans and Vichy Carrots with Fresh Ginger, plus indulgent Creamy Potato Gratin and Baked Spinach Mornay. And who says a salad is just for summer? Use quality seasonal produce to create light meals or accompaniments such as Butternut Squash and Pancetta Salad with Mixed Spice Dressing and Winter-spiced Salad with Pears, Honeyed Pecans, and Ricotta.

Baking is such a satisfying and comforting pastime as well as being very cost-effective. Make a batch of Stem Ginger Cookies and fill the barrel so that family can help themselves during the week. Keep a Sticky Marzipan and Cherry Loaf in the cake tin and offer visitors who come in from the cold a slice of something home-baked with a warming cup of coffee.

Finally, you'll find a tempting array of warming drinks guaranteed to stave off the winter blues. Included are flavored coffees, spiced teas, indulgent hot chocolates, and milky bedtime drinks and, as it's the party season, plenty of recipes for punches and cocktails. Try traditional tipples such as Egg Nog and Orange-mulled Wine or choose from a selection of elegant cocktails—Brandy Alexander, White Russian, or a sparkling Champagne cocktail— all guaranteed to bring some festive cheer to the coldest of winter evenings.

soups and snacks

chestnut and Puy lentil soup with whipped celeriac cream

This is a spectacularly rich, satisfying soup with a light-as-air, foamy topping. You can prepare the soup ahead and it's a particularly good way to use up a tasty turkey or ham stock. You don't have to peel your own chestnuts, but they do taste wonderful and it's a nice, cozy thing to do if you've got company in the kitchen. If you prefer to serve the soup on its own without the celeriac cream, save some of the chopped chestnut for garnishing, frying the pieces in a little butter and sprinkling over the soup before serving.

12 oz. peeled chestnuts (fresh or vacuum-packed)

4 tablespoons light olive oil

1 leek, trimmed and thinly sliced

1 large carrot, finely diced

1 celery rib, thinly sliced

1 garlic clove, crushed

1 teaspoon Spanish sweet paprika (pimentón dulce) or paprika

1½–2 quarts fresh turkey, duck, ham, chicken, or game stock or stock made with 2 beef or chicken stock cubes

1 cup green Puy lentils, rinsed

2 tablespoons dry Marsala, Madeira, or amontillado sherry

½–1 teaspoon Worcestershire or dark soy sauce

sea salt and freshly ground black pepper

celeriac cream

1 lb. celeriac

2⅓ cups low-fat milk

2 tablespoons butter

freshly grated nutmeg, to taste

freshly snipped chives, to garnish

Serves 6–8

Wash the chestnuts and make a cut with a sharp knife in the curved side of each one. Put in a saucepan of boiling water, bring back to a boil and boil for 3 minutes. Turn the heat off and remove the chestnuts 2 at a time, letting them cool for a few seconds, then peeling off both the hard outer shell and inner brown papery skin. If they become harder to peel, bring the water back to a boil again. Chop the chestnuts roughly.

Heat the oil in a large saucepan, add the leek, carrot, and celery, stir well and cook over medium heat until the vegetables start to soften (about 5–6 minutes). Stir in the garlic and pimentón and cook for a minute, then add the chestnuts and 1 quart of the stock and bring to a boil. Add the lentils to the vegetables, then cook for about 35–40 minutes until the vegetables are soft. Cool for 10 minutes, then pass the soup in batches through a food processor. Return the soup and remaining stock to the pan, add the Marsala and reheat

gently. Add more stock if necessary and season to taste with salt, pepper, and Worcestershire sauce.

Meanwhile, to make the celeriac cream, remove the tough outer skin from the celeriac and cut it into cubes. Put in a saucepan, add enough of the milk to cover and bring to a boil. Partially cover the pan and simmer for about 20–25 minutes, until the celeriac is soft. Remove the celeriac with a slotted spoon, leaving the liquid behind, and whizz it in a food processor. Season with salt, pepper, and a little freshly grated nutmeg. Remove half the purée and add half the remaining milk to the purée in the food processor. Whizz until smooth, light, and foamy, adding the extra milk if needed.

Serve the soup in bowls with a generous swirl of celeriac purée on the top and garnish with snipped chives. Serve with some crusty sourdough or multigrain bread.

pumpkin soup
with honey and sage

This is based on a delicious soup that is served at a London restaurant called Tom's Kitchen, run by top chef Tom Aikens. His version contains chicken stock but this recipe is vegetarian, but you could base it on chicken stock too.

5 tablespoons unsalted butter

1 small–medium onion, roughly chopped

1 carrot, finely chopped

1 garlic clove, crushed

2¼ lbs. pumpkin or butternut squash, seeded, peeled, and cut into cubes

2 heaping tablespoons clear honey

3 sprigs of sage, plus extra crisp-fried leaves (optional), to serve

3 cups vegetable stock

⅓ cup heavy cream

freshly squeezed lemon juice, to taste

sea salt and freshly ground black pepper

Serves 4–6

Gently melt the butter in a large lidded saucepan or flameproof casserole dish. Add the onion, carrot, and garlic. Stir, cover and cook over low heat for about 4–5 minutes. Add the pumpkin, honey, and sage, stir, replace the lid and continue to cook very gently for about 10 minutes. Pour in the stock, bring to a boil and cook for a further 10 minutes until the vegetables are soft. Turn off the heat and allow the soup to cool slightly, then remove the sage and strain the soup, retaining the liquid. Put half the cooked vegetables in a food processor with just enough of the reserved cooking liquid to blend into a smooth purée.

Transfer to a clean saucepan and repeat with the remaining vegetables, adding the purée to the first batch. Whizz the remaining liquid in the food processor to pick up the last bits of purée and add that too. Bring the soup slowly to a boil, then stir in the cream without boiling further. Season to taste with lemon juice, salt, and pepper.

Serve with an extra swirl of cream or scatter some crisp-fried sage leaves on top, and serve with whole-meal or multigrain bread.

roasted tomato soup with rarebit toasts

This hearty homemade tomato soup packs a real flavor punch. It's very easy to make and much, much tastier than any store-bought versions. It's also highly nutritious, packed with antioxidants and therefore one of the best remedies to help fight off winter colds and coughs. Roasting the tomatoes does add to the cooking time but it's well worth the effort as something magical happens during the roasting process and the flavor is concentrated, retaining the natural sweetness of fresh tomatoes. The rarebit toasts are a deliciously indulgent addition but the soup can be more simply served with a swirl of cream or crème fraîche if preferred.

2¼ lbs. Italian tomatoes, such as Roma, halved

2 small red onions, quartered

6 sprigs of lemon thyme

1 teaspoon sugar

1 teaspoon sea salt

2 garlic cloves, sliced

2 tablespoons olive oil

2 cups vegetable stock

sea salt and freshly ground black pepper

rarebit toasts

4 oz. sharp cheddar cheese

3 tablespoons wheat beer

1 tablespoon Worcestershire sauce

4 slices of baguette

Serves 4

Preheat the oven to 325°F. Put the tomatoes, onion, lemon thyme, sugar, salt, garlic, and oil in a large bowl. Use your hands to toss the ingredients to combine and evenly coat them in the oil. Tip the mixture out onto a baking sheet and roast in the preheated oven for 1½ hours. Discard the lemon thyme sprigs then put the tomatoes, onions, and any tasty juices in a food processor or blender and process until smooth, adding a little stock if the mixture is too thick to process. Transfer to a large saucepan, add the stock, and cook over gentle heat for 10 minutes. Season to taste and keep warm.

Preheat the broiler to high. Put the cheddar, beer, and Worcestershire sauce in a small saucepan and set over low heat. Stir until the cheese has melted and the mixture is smooth. Toast the bread under the hot broiler on one side only. Spread about 2 tablespoons of the cheese mixture on each untoasted side of bread and broil until it is bubbling and golden. Ladle the soup into warmed serving bowls and sit a rarebit toast on top of each to serve.

slow-cooked onion and cider soup
with Gruyère toasts

Alongside tomatoes, onions are almost certainly the most important ingredient in the kitchen. They are so versatile and give depth of flavor to so many dishes. The sweet onion mixture here could also be added to an egg custard and baked in a pastry shell with some soft goat cheese to make a savory tart, or spread on a pizza base and topped with black olives and fresh thyme.

3 tablespoons butter

2¼ lbs. yellow onions, thinly sliced

4 garlic cloves

4 cups vegetable stock

1½ cups hard sweet cider

2 egg yolks

4 thin slices of baguette

4 oz. Gruyère cheese, thinly sliced

Serves 4

Put the butter in a saucepan and set over medium heat. Add the onions and garlic, partially cover with a lid, and cook for 20 minutes, stirring often so that the onions become silky soft without burning. Add the stock and cider and bring to a boil. Reduce the heat to low and cook for about 40 minutes, until thick and golden. Remove from the heat and slowly whisk in the egg yolks. Cover and keep warm.

Preheat the broiler to high. Toast the bread under the hot broiler until lightly golden on one side only. Put the cheese slices on the untoasted side and grill until the cheese is golden brown and bubbling. Ladle the soup into warmed serving bowls and sit a Gruyère toast on top of each to serve.

spicy red vegetable soup

The color of this fiery red vegetable soup is matched by a pleasing chile kick, which can be adjusted according to your palate—just add extra chiles as required. It's a really rewarding recipe so don't be put off by the cooking time.

¼ cup light olive oil

1 tablespoon soft brown sugar

1 red bell pepper, seeded and chopped

2¼ lbs. Roma or plum tomatoes, quartered

1 red onion, chopped

1 large red chile, seeded and chopped

2 garlic cloves, chopped

1 cup vegetable or chicken stock

4 slices of rye bread

2 oz. soft goat cheese

Serves 4

Preheat the oven to 350°F.

Put the olive oil, sugar, bell pepper, tomatoes, onion, chile, and garlic in a roasting pan and use your hands to toss until coated in oil. Cook in the preheated oven for 2 hours, turning often, until the vegetables are really soft and starting to turn brown.

Remove the vegetables from the oven. Put the stock in a saucepan and add the vegetables. Spoon the mixture, in batches, into a food processor or blender and process until smooth. Return the soup to a clean saucepan and warm over low heat for a few minutes until heated through.

Toast the rye bread and, while it's still warm, spread over the cheese. Ladle the soup into warmed serving bowls and sit a soft cheese toast on top of each to serve.

creamy cauliflower and Gruyère soup

Try and find a small, whole head of cauliflower that is creamy-white and soft for this indulgent soup. This recipe does not involve straining the puréed mixture (a messy and laborious job) so you want to avoid cooking with a gnarly, old head for a good result.

2 tablespoons butter

1 white onion, roughly chopped

1 celery rib, chopped

1 small cauliflower, about 2 lbs., cut into small pieces

1.5 quarts vegetable or chicken stock

1 cup heavy cream

2 cups grated Gruyère cheese, plus extra to serve

sea salt and freshly ground black pepper

freshly chopped parsley and toasted whole-wheat bread, to serve

Serves 4

Heat the butter in a saucepan set over high heat. Add the onion and celery and cook for 5 minutes, until the onion has softened but not browned.

Add the cauliflower pieces and stock and bring to a boil. Let boil for 25–30 minutes, until the cauliflower is really soft and breaking up in the stock.

Transfer the mixture to a food processor or blender and process in batches until smooth. Return the purée to a clean saucepan. Add the cream and cheese and cook over low heat, stirring constantly, until the cheese has all smoothly melted into the soup.

Season to taste with a little salt and pepper. Ladle into warmed serving bowls. Serve sprinkled with chopped parsley and extra grated cheese with whole-wheat toast on the side.

carrot and lentil soup

You'll need to use a variety of lentil here that will soften to a mush when cooked for a short time. French green lentils, or Puy, will not work. Orange or red varieties are what's needed and they also create the rich color. The taste of this soup belies the simplicity of its ingredients. Carrots can be very sweet and lentils are nutty and wholesome so they make a perfect pair. Try adding a couple of tablespoons of mild curry powder to the onions at the early stage of cooking.

3 tablespoons butter

1 red onion, chopped

1 garlic clove, chopped

2 tablespoons sun-dried tomato paste

1 lb. carrots, peeled and grated

1¼ cups red lentils, rinsed

1½ quarts chicken or vegetable stock

½ cup plain yogurt

a handful of cilantro leaves, chopped

Serves 4

Heat the butter in a large saucepan set over high heat. Add the onion and garlic and cook for 4–5 minutes, stirring often. Add the sun-dried tomato paste and stir-fry for 1 minute. Add the carrots, lentils, and stock to the pan and bring to a boil. Cook at a rapid simmer for 40 minutes, until the lentils are soft.

Spoon the mixture, in batches, into a food processor or blender and process until smooth. Return the soup to the saucepan and warm over low heat.

Ladle the soup into warmed serving bowls and serve with a dollop of yogurt and a sprinkling of chopped cilantro.

classic lamb, chickpea, and lentil soup with cumin

Variations of this soup can be found throughout the Islamic world. In Morocco alone there are at least a dozen versions of this soup, differentiated by their regional recipes and by the legumes and vegetables used in the soup. It is one of the classic dishes prepared at religious feasts and it is traditionally served to break the fast during Ramadan, the month of fasting. Thick and hearty, with a consistency that comes somewhere between a soup and a stew, it can be served as a meal on its own with thick, crusty bread or flat breads.

Heat the oil in a deep, heavy-based saucepan. Add the onions, celery, and carrots and cook until the onions begin to color. Add the garlic and cumin seeds and toss in the lamb. Cook until lightly browned. Add the spices, sugar, and bay leaves and stir in the tomato paste. Pour in the stock and bring the liquid to a boil. Reduce the heat, cover with a lid, and simmer for 1 hour, until the meat is tender.

Add the chopped tomatoes, chickpeas, and lentils to the pan and cook gently for a further 30 minutes, until the lentils are soft and the soup is almost as thick as a stew. Top up with a little water, if necessary, as the lentils will absorb most of it. Season the soup with salt and pepper and add most of the parsley and cilantro.

Serve the soup piping hot, sprinkled with the remaining parsley and cilantro and with wedges of lemon to squeeze over it and plenty of bread for dipping.

2–3 tablespoons olive oil

2 yellow onions, chopped

2 celery ribs, diced

2 small carrots, peeled and diced

2–3 garlic cloves, left whole but smashed

1 tablespoon cumin seeds

1 lb. lean lamb, cut into bite-size cubes

2–3 teaspoons ground turmeric

2 teaspoons paprika

2 teaspoons ground cinnamon

2 teaspoons sugar

2 fresh or dry bay leaves

2 tablespoons tomato paste

4 cups lamb or chicken stock

14-oz. can chickpeas, drained and rinsed

14-oz. can chopped tomatoes, drained of juice

⅔ cup brown or green lentils, rinsed

a small bunch of flatleaf parsley, chopped

a small bunch of cilantro, chopped

sea salt and freshly ground black pepper

1 lemon, cut into quarters, to garnish

Serves 4–6

potato, bacon, and Savoy cabbage soup

This hearty recipe was inspired by a Polish soup called zurek which uses a fermented flour batter. This simplified recipes uses fine oatmeal instead but it still thickens the soup up very nicely.

2 tablespoons extra virgin olive oil

8 slices of thick-cut smoked bacon, chopped

1 yellow onion, chopped

2 garlic cloves, crushed

⅛ teaspoon ground allspice

10 oz. potatoes, peeled and cubed

¼ Savoy cabbage, shredded

1⅔ cups chicken or vegetable stock

1⅔ cups milk

2 tablespoons fine oatmeal

freshly ground black pepper

Serves 4

Heat the olive oil in a heavy-based saucepan or casserole dish. Add the bacon and fry for 2–3 minutes, until cooked. Turn the heat down and add the onion and garlic. Cover and cook for about 3 minutes, or until the onion is starting to soften.

Add the allspice and potatoes, cover and cook for a further 2–3 minutes to start softening the potatoes. Add the cabbage and stir until it has wilted into the rest of the ingredients. Pour in the stock and milk and bring to a boil.

Mix the oatmeal with 3–4 tablespoons cold water until smooth and gradually whisk into the soup to thicken.

Ladle the soup into warmed serving bowls and grind over some black pepper to serve.

parsnip, chorizo, and chestnut soup

This is a thick and unctuous soup; the kind you want to wolf down after a long walk or building a snowman in the depths of winter. It's very heavy so a little goes a long way; it can be served as a meal in itself—offering it as an appetizer is likely to leave anyone too full-up for another course!

4 oz. raw chorizo, cubed

1 yellow onion, chopped

3 garlic cloves, sliced

1 celery rib, chopped

1 carrot, peeled and chopped

3 parsnips, peeled and chopped

¼ teaspoon dried hot pepper flakes

1 teaspoon ground cumin

7 oz. peeled, cooked chestnuts
(fresh or vacuum-packed)

4 cups chicken, ham, or vegetable stock

sea salt and freshly ground black pepper

Serves 4–6

Put the chorizo in a large saucepan and heat gently for 2–3 minutes until the oil seeps out and the chorizo becomes slightly crispy. Lift out the chorizo with a slotted spoon, trying to leave as much oil behind as you can and set to one side.

Add the onion, garlic, celery, carrot, and parsnips to the pan, stir well, cover and cook gently for 10 minutes, or until softening. Add the dried hot pepper flakes and cumin, season well with salt and pepper and stir to release the aroma. Add the chestnuts and hot stock, then cover and simmer over low heat for 25–30 minutes until everything is very tender.

Transfer the contents of the pan to a blender (or use a handheld blender) and liquidize until smooth. Reheat the chorizo in a small skillet.

Ladle the soup into warmed serving bowls and scatter with the crispy chorizo to serve.

monkfish, fennel, and saffron bourride

A bourride is a little like a bouillabaisse but thickened with a gorgeous, garlicky aïoli. The aïoli in this recipe is spiced up with harissa, a Moroccan chile and spice paste (see note on page 61), and is heavenly spread on anything. It's an impressive soup for dinner parties and can be served as an entrée if liked.

3 tablespoons olive oil

1 white onion, chopped

1 fennel bulb, finely chopped

1 leek, white part sliced

10 oz. new potatoes (unpeeled), thinly sliced

¼ teaspoon saffron threads

2 fresh thyme sprigs

2 large tomatoes, thinly sliced

1¼ lbs. monkfish fillets, skinned and sliced

4 cups fish stock

sea salt and freshly ground black pepper

toasted bread, to serve

¾ cup finely grated Gruyère cheese, to serve

harissa aïoli

2 egg yolks

1 teaspoon Dijon mustard

¾ cup extra virgin olive oil

2 garlic cloves, crushed

2 teaspoons harissa paste

1 tablespoon freshly squeezed lemon juice

Serves 4–6

Heat the olive oil in a large saucepan set over low heat. Add the onion, fennel, and leek and cook for 5 minutes. Add the potatoes, saffron, and thyme, stirring just once or twice, and cook until the potatoes start to soften.

Add the tomatoes and monkfish in a layer on top and, without stirring, pour in the stock. It should come at least halfway up the fish; if not, top up with water. Bring to a boil over gentle heat with the lid on and cook for 10–12 minutes until the fish is cooked and the potatoes are tender.

Meanwhile, to make the aïoli, put the egg yolks and mustard in a mixing bowl and whisk with electric beaters. Trickle in the olive oil, whisking until it emulsifies and thickens. Season with salt and pepper, then stir in the garlic, harissa, and lemon juice. Transfer half the aïoli to a serving small dish.

Siphon off 2–3 ladlefuls of the liquid in the saucepan, add it to the remaining aïoli, and stir well until combined. Stir back into the saucepan. Warm over low heat and season to taste, but don't allow the soup to reach a boil.

Ladle the soup into warmed serving bowls and serve with toast, extra aïoli, and finely grated Gruyère on the side.

Note The aïoli contains raw eggs, see note on page 4.

smoked haddock and bean soup

Smoked haddock provides that warm smoky flavor that cold wintry nights call for. Beans are a perfect ingredient for soups—they are so quick and easy to throw in and thicken soups up nicely. Here a combination of cannellini and butter beans is used.

4 tablespoons olive oil

1 red onion, thinly sliced

2½ cups fish stock

3 fresh or dried bay leaves

finely grated peel of 1 lemon

10 oz. smoked haddock, skinned and cubed

14-oz. can cannellini beans, drained and rinsed

14-oz. can butter beans, drained and rinsed

4 tablespoons crème fraîche or sour cream

water or milk, to thin (optional)

sea salt and freshly ground black pepper

Serves 4

Heat the olive oil in a large saucepan and add the onion. Fry for 1 minute then cover and cook over low heat for 10 minutes, stirring every now and then until soft.

Pour in the stock, add the bay leaves and grated lemon peel and bring to a gentle simmer. Add the smoked haddock and cook for 3–4 minutes until opaque. It will continue to cook in the residual heat.

Liquidize half the cannellini beans and half the butter beans with ¾ cup water in a blender and stir into the soup. Stir in the remaining whole beans and add the crème fraîche. Season with salt. If the soup is too thick, add a little milk or water to thin it down.

Ladle the soup into warmed serving bowls and grind over some black pepper to serve.

leek and potato soup

Sometimes the classics are the best and with leek and potato this is certainly true. If you are using nice clean leeks, you can slice them lengthwise and simply rinse them under the faucet, but if you are lucky enough to have some from the garden place them in a sink full of warm water and swirl them around to dissolve the mud and encourage it to come out.

3 tablespoons butter

4 leeks (about 1 lb.), chopped

3 floury potatoes (about 8 oz.), peeled and chopped

1 white onion, finely chopped

2 cups vegetable stock

1¼ cups milk

2 dried bay leaves

2 tablespoons freshly snipped chives, to serve

sea salt and freshly ground black pepper

Serves 4–6

Melt the butter in a large, heavy-based saucepan and add the leeks, potatoes, onion, and a large pinch of salt. Cover and cook over low heat for 15 minutes until soft and translucent. Stir occasionally so that the vegetables don't catch on the bottom of the pan.

Add the stock, milk, and bay leaves and bring to a boil. Turn the heat down and simmer, covered, for 20 minutes until the potato is so soft it is falling apart.

Transfer the soup to a blender, removing the bay leaves as you unearth them, and liquidize until smooth. Strain the blended soup through a strainer back into the pan to get it extra smooth and velvety. Bring back to a boil.

Ladle the soup into warmed serving bowls, scatter with chives, and add a few grinds of black pepper to serve.

mushroom soup with Madeira and hazelnuts

The earthiness of mushrooms blends well with the sweetness of Madeira wine. The hazelnuts add a thickness to the soup and another complimentary flavor, but you can omit them if you prefer.

3 tablespoons butter

1 large yellow onion, chopped

3 garlic cloves, crushed

3 tablespoons blanched hazelnuts

3 tablespoons freshly chopped parsley

12 oz. brown or cremini mushrooms, sliced

1 oz. dried porcini mushrooms

6 tablespoons Madeira

4 cups vegetable or chicken stock, warmed

Serves 4–6

Melt the butter in a large saucepan and add the onion and garlic. Cover and cook over low heat for 10 minutes, or until soft. Stir occasionally so that they don't color. Meanwhile, toast the hazelnuts in a dry skillet and roughly chop, then set aside.

Add half the parsley and all the mushrooms to the saucepan and turn the heat up to medium. Cover and cook, stirring, for about 15 minutes until they are softened.

Put the dried mushrooms in a heatproof bowl with ½ cup of the hot stock and set aside to

soak for about 15 minutes to rehydrate.

Add the Madeira to the pan and cook until it evaporates. Add the remaining stock and the dried mushrooms with their soaking liquid, cover and cook for 10 minutes.

Transfer half the soup to a blender, along with half the hazelnuts and liquidize until smooth, then stir back into the pan and heat through.

Ladle the soup into warmed serving bowls and scatter the remaining parsley and toasted hazelnuts over the top to serve.

oven-roasted spiced nuts

This recipe gives you control of the salt, the type of nut, and the spice mix. When cool, mix in anything else you fancy, such as dried fruits or seeds.

3 tablespoons unsalted butter

1 tablespoon Indian garam masala, Chinese five-spice, Cajun, or other spice mix, hot or mild

1 egg white

1 lb. mixed skinned nuts, such as almonds, Brazils, hazelnuts, and pecans

1 teaspoon fine sea salt

Makes about 1 lb.

Preheat the oven to 300°F. Melt the butter in a small saucepan and stir in the spices. Let cool slightly, then whisk in the egg white until foamy. Add the nuts and toss well to coat. Spread the nuts out evenly in a thin layer in a roasting pan and roast slowly in the preheated oven for 30 minutes to 1 hour, stirring from time to time, until they are golden and toasted. Remove from the oven and toss the nuts with the salt.

Let cool completely, then store for at least 1 day before eating. They will keep in an airtight container for up to 2 weeks.

Parmesan and rosemary wafers

These are a must for any good drinks party, as the crispness of the cheese is wonderful and the infusion of the rosemary divine. Everyone will be constantly nibbling, so make lots. They can be prepared in advance but must be kept chilled in an airtight container until you are ready to serve.

2 sprigs of rosemary, needles stripped and finely chopped

8 oz. Parmesan cheese, coarsely grated

2 baking sheets, lined with non-stick baking parchment

Makes 24

Preheat the oven to 400°F. Put the rosemary into a bowl and stir in the Parmesan. Put teaspoons of the mixture in little heaps on the baking sheets and flatten out into circles, making sure that they are not too close, as they will spread. Bake in the preheated oven for 8–10 minutes until golden, remove and let cool. Gently peel off the paper and serve.

dukkah

No Egyptian home is complete without a jar of this wonderful seed and nut mixture in the pantry. It is normally eaten as a snack—bread is dipped first into olive oil, then into the dukkah. Serve it with breadsticks and the most delicious olive oil you can find. It is also great used as a coating for chicken or fish instead of bread crumbs.

1 cup whole shelled hazelnuts

⅔ cup whole shelled almonds

⅔ cup sesame seeds

½ cup coriander seeds

½ cup ground cumin

1 teaspoon sea salt

½ teaspoon freshly ground black pepper

to serve

extra virgin olive oil

breadsticks or strips of toasted flatbread

Makes about 3½ cups

Preheat the oven to 400°F. Put the hazelnuts, almonds, and sesame seeds in an ovenproof dish in the preheated oven and toast for 5–10 minutes. Remove from the oven, then tip onto a plate to cool completely. If they aren't cool enough, they will turn oily when ground.

Toast the coriander seeds in a dry skillet for 1–2 minutes until you can smell the aroma, tip onto the cooling nuts, then add the ground cumin to the pan. Toast for 30 seconds then transfer to the plate.

When cold, put the nuts, spices, salt, and pepper in a food processor and blend to a coarse, powdery meal—still dry-looking, but not totally pulverized. Spoon into a bowl and serve with a bowl of olive oil and breadsticks or flatbread cut into strips.

beef and ale pâté

This spicy pâté is real party fare. It was inspired by "tinga," Mexican shredded beef, and relies on slow cooking and a few key flavors. Even though it calls for a cheap cut of beef, it pays to use the best quality you can find. Serve it as you would a dip.

¾ cup dried pinto beans

2 tablespoons olive oil

5 large, mild red chiles

3 whole garlic cloves, peeled

1 large, dried mulatto or ancho chile (optional)

1¼ lbs. blade steak, trimmed of fat and cut into 1-inch chunks

2 x 12-oz. bottles of ale

sea salt and freshly ground black pepper

8 tablespoons chopped cilantro, to garnish

plain tortilla chips, to serve

Serves 4–6

Soak the beans in cold water overnight. Drain, put in a saucepan, and cover with plenty of water. Bring to a boil and continue to boil for 10 minutes. Drain the beans and set aside.

Heat the olive oil in a large, heavy-based saucepan set over medium/low heat. Cut the green stalk ends from 3 of the red chiles. Put these chiles and the garlic in the saucepan and gently cook for 3 minutes. If using, cut the dried chile in half and remove the seeds and stalk. Add the flesh to the saucepan and continue cooking for 2 minutes. Increase the heat to medium/high, add the steak and cook, stirring occasionally, for 5 minutes until the meat is browned.

Add the ale and beans to the saucepan and bring to a boil. Reduce the heat to a slow simmer, cover, and cook for 1½ hours, stirring occasionally. Uncover the pan and cook for 1 hour until the meat is falling apart. Put the meat with its accompanying ingredients and a little of the cooking liquid in a food processor and process briefly until you have a coarse pâté. Season to taste.

Spoon into serving dishes. Cut the remaining red chiles into thin strips and scatter over the pâté with the cilantro. Serve warm or at room temperature with plain tortilla chips.

trio of honey-baked camembert with calvados and herbs

3 x 8-oz. boxes of Camembert cheese

3 tablespoons calvados or brandy

3 tablespoons dark honey

1 garlic clove, sliced

3 fresh sage leaves

3 sprigs of fresh rosemary

3 fresh bay leaves

to serve

celery ribs

walnut bread

chilled tiny radishes

Serves about 15

Another great recipe for entertaining, this molten cheese dish is spiked with perfumed honey, pungent calvados, and garlic. Serve with crunchy celery ribs, warm crusty walnut bread, and chilled radishes for dipping.

Preheat the oven to 400°F.

Unwrap the cheeses and return them to their boxes. Using a skewer, make 6 or 7 holes in each cheese. Mix the calvados and honey together and spoon the mixture into and over the holes. Stud with the garlic slices and lightly press the sage, rosemary, and bay leaves onto each cheese. Bake in the preheated oven for about 7 minutes.

Remove the boxes from the oven. Using sharp scissors, quickly make 3 cuts on the surface of each cheese, from the center out, and gently open the "petals" a little. Take the cheeses out of their boxes, put them on a cheeseboard or plate, and serve straight away, with the celery ribs, walnut bread, and radishes on the side for dipping.

trio of vegetable dips with spelt toasts

Have you ever been lucky enough to share a plate of mixed dips at a Turkish restaurant? It's the vibrant colors that first grab your attention, quickly followed by the delicious flavors. These dips are all made with root vegetables, all too often lurking at the bottom of your veggie box. They have a creamy texture, so the crisp toasts are a nice nutty contrast.

spelt toasts

¾ cup spelt, rinsed under cold water

1 tablespoon active dry yeast

2 cups spelt flour

½ teaspoon fine sea salt

all-purpose flour, for dusting

Makes about 40 toasts

Put the spelt in a saucepan with 4 cups water and bring to a boil. Reduce the heat to low, cover with a lid and cook for 45 minutes. Remove the lid and boil rapidly until almost all the liquid has evaporated.

Meanwhile, put the yeast in a bowl with 4 tablespoons warm water, stir, cover, and let rest in a warm place until the mixture is frothy. While it is still warm, put the spelt in a bowl with the spelt flour, salt, ½ cup hand-hot water, and the yeast and stir to bring the mixture together to form a sticky dough. Put the dough on a lightly floured work surface and gently knead for about 1 minute. Carefully transfer the dough to a lightly oiled bowl, cover with a kitchen towel, and let rise in a warm place for 1–1¼ hours, until it has doubled in size.

Preheat the oven to 400°F. Tip the dough out onto a lightly oiled baking sheet and, using floured hands, form the dough into a loaf. Bake the bread in the preheated oven for 40 minutes. Carefully slide the loaf off the baking sheet and directly onto the oven shelf, then bake for a further 5 minutes. Remove from the oven and let cool. To serve, slice into ¼-inch wide pieces and toast under a hot broiler until golden and crispy on both sides.

roasted parsnip and garlic dip

2 tablespoons chilled butter, cubed • ⅓ cup heavy cream • ½ teaspoon
sea salt • ¼ teaspoon white pepper • 1 lb. parsnips, peeled and sliced •
1 garlic bulb, cut in half

Serves 6–8

Preheat the oven to 350°F. Lightly butter a small baking dish. Put the
cream in a bowl and add the salt and pepper. Put the parsnips in the
dish with the garlic. Pour the cream over the top, cover with foil,
and cook in the preheated oven for 45 minutes.

Remove the garlic and let cool. When cool enough to handle,
squeeze the garlic directly into the bowl of a blender and discard
the skin. Add the remaining ingredients and process until smooth.
Transfer to a dish and cover until ready to serve.

beet and caraway dip

3 medium beets, uncooked • 1 tablespoon horseradish sauce •
⅓ cup sour cream • 1 teaspoon caraway seeds • sea salt and white pepper

Serves 6–8

Put the beets in a large saucepan and cover with cold water.
Bring to a boil and let boil for 45–50 minutes, until tender and
easily pierced with a skewer. Drain and let cool. When cool enough
to handle, peel and discard the skins. Roughly chop and put in
a blender with the other ingredients and process until smooth.
Season to taste, transfer to a dish, and cover until ready to serve.

spiced carrot dip

1 cup vegetable stock • 4 medium carrots, chopped • 2 tablespoons
light olive oil • 1 small red onion, chopped • 2 garlic cloves, chopped •
1 large red chile, chopped • 1 teaspoon fenugreek seeds • 1 teaspoon
ground cumin • sea salt and white pepper

Serves 6–8

Put the stock in a saucepan, add the carrots, oil, onion, and garlic.
and bring to a boil. Reduce the heat to low and simmer for 15–20
minutes, until almost all the liquid has evaporated and the carrots
are soft. Add the chile, fenugreek, and cumin and cook for 2 minutes.
Put in a blender and process until blended but with a rough texture.
Season to taste, transfer to a dish, and cover until ready to serve.

warm cheese scones with cheddar and pickled pears

These little scones are particularly good served warm and
filled at the last minute. If you have any leftover pickled pears
you could serve them with cold meats or a cheese platter.
Gruyère could be substituted for the cheddar if liked.

pickled pears

1½ lbs. firm pears

1½ cups soft brown sugar

2 cups cider vinegar

½ onion studded with 4 cloves

2 fresh bay leaves, bruised

1 cinnamon stick

cheese scones

3¾ cups self-rising flour, plus
extra for dusting

1 stick plus 2 tablespoons butter

1 cup grated sharp cheddar cheese

2 teaspoons salt

2 teaspoons baking soda

1 teaspoon Dijon mustard

1 teaspoon cayenne pepper

¾ cup milk

7 oz. sharp cheddar cheese,
shaved into thin slices

a 1½-inch cookie cutter (optional)

2 –3 baking sheets

Makes 30 small scones

To make the pickled pears, peel, quarter, and core the pears. Put all
the other ingredients in a large saucepan and gently bring to a boil.
When the sugar has dissolved, add the pears and simmer for about
5–8 minutes until just tender. Remove the pears from the liquid with
a slotted spoon and transfer them to a shallow dish. Set aside to cool.

Continue boiling the liquid until it reduces by half and becomes a
syrup. Discard the onion, bay leaves, and cinnamon and gently pour
the syrup over the pears to coat.

To make the scones, preheat the oven to 400°F. Rub the flour and
butter together in a bowl until it resembles fine bread crumbs then
add ½ cup of the grated cheese. Add the salt, baking soda, mustard,
and cayenne pepper and mix to combine. Next add enough milk to
bring the dry ingredients together and form a pliable dough. Flour a
work surface, turn the dough out and knead it lightly. Pat it out to
a thickness of ½ inch. Use a cookie cutter or an unturned glass to
stamp out small rounds. Sprinkle the remaining grated cheese over
the scones, transfer to baking sheets and bake for 10 minutes until
lightly browned. Let cool a little on a wire rack.

Slice the pickled pears into small pieces. Cut the scones three
quarters of the way through, put a slice of cheese and a piece of
pickled pear inside each one and serve immediately.

potato and parsnip croquettes

Use a floury potato for these croquettes, such as Desirée, as it fluffs up nicely when boiled and mashed. The parsnip adds an interesting flavor dimension, as it is a little bitter and sweet at the same time. Serve warm with mild mustard on the side for dipping.

1 lb. floury potatoes, peeled and quartered

1 parsnip, peeled and quartered

3 tablespoons butter, plus 1 tablespoon for frying

2 tablespoons finely chopped parsley

2 eggs

1 cup dry bread crumbs from a day-old loaf of bread

2 tablespoons all-purpose flour, for dusting

vegetable oil, for shallow-frying

sea salt and freshly ground black pepper

sweet German mustard, to serve

Makes 18 croquettes

Put the potatoes and parsnip in a large saucepan and cover with boiling water. Set over high heat and boil for 12–15 minutes until tender. Drain and return to the warm pan. Add 2 tablespoons of the butter and mash well until the mixture is lump-free. Stir in the parsley and season well with salt and pepper. Cover and refrigerate until the mixture is completely chilled.

Break the eggs into a bowl and beat well to combine. Put the bread crumbs in a separate bowl. Lightly flour your hands and work surface. Take 1 heaping tablespoon of mixture and form it into a small sausage, tapping the ends on the floured work surface so that they are flattened rather than tapered. Dip the croquette in the beaten egg, then roll it in the crumbs until coated. Put it on a baking sheet lined with baking parchment. Repeat until all of the potato mixture has been used and then chill until ready to cook.

Put the remaining tablespoon of butter in a skillet and pour in sufficient oil to come halfway up the sides of the pan. Heat the pan over medium heat until the butter begins to sizzle. To test if the oil is hot enough, sprinkle a few bread crumbs into it—they should sizzle on contact. Cook the croquettes in batches for 2–3 minutes, turning often, until golden and crisp all over. Remove from the oil using a slotted spoon and drain on paper towels to remove excess oil. Serve warm with the mustard on the side for dipping.

crispy onion rings
with Parmesan aïoli

These are a good thing to cook at the same time as the croquettes (see recipe left), especially if you don't cook fried food often. You don't have to be too fussy and cook one ring at a time—they taste just as delicious cooked in clumps. Enjoy them warm with the aïoli on the side for dipping.

2 red onions, sliced into ¼-inch thick rings

2 yellow onions, sliced into ¼-inch thick rings

1 cup buttermilk (or 1 cup full-fat milk combined with 1 tablespoon freshly squeezed lemon juice)

6 tablespoons chickpea flour

6 tablespoons cornstarch

1 teaspoon sea salt

2 eggs

2 cups vegetable oil

Parmesan aïoli

2 egg yolks

2 garlic cloves, crushed

2 teaspoons freshly squeezed lemon juice

¾ cup light olive oil

¼ cup very finely grated Parmesan cheese

sea salt and white pepper

Serves 4

To make the aïoli, put the egg yolks, garlic, and lemon juice in a small bowl and whisk until just combined. Whisk constantly as you add the oil, very slowly at first but building up to a steady stream. Stir in the Parmesan and season with salt and pepper. Set aside.

Put the onion slices in a large bowl and gently toss to separate the rings. Add the buttermilk and stir. Set aside for 1 hour. Put the chickpea flour, cornstarch, and salt in a bowl. Make a small well in the center. Use a slotted spoon to remove the onions from the buttermilk (reserving the buttermilk) and transfer them to a colander to drain off any excess liquid. Put ½ cup of the reserved buttermilk in

a bowl and beat in the eggs until just combined. Pour this mixture into the flour mixture and beat well with a wooden spoon to form a smooth, thick batter.

Put the oil in a skillet and set over medium/high heat. Toss a handful of onion rings into the batter and lift them out with a slotted spoon (letting any excess batter drip back into the bowl.) Put them in the skillet. Cook for about 1–2 minutes, until crisp and golden. Remove from the oil with a slotted spoon and drain on paper towels. Repeat with the remaining onion rings. Serve hot with the Parmesan aïoli on the side for dipping.

2 teaspoons butter

2 teaspoons all-purpose flour

½ cup full-fat milk

½ cup finely grated Manchego cheese

12 wide, flat mushrooms

¼ teaspoon Spanish smoked paprika (pimentón)

fennel salad

1 small fennel bulb

1 handful of flatleaf parsley leaves

2 teaspoons extra virgin olive oil

2 teaspoons freshly squeezed lemon juice

sea salt and freshly ground black pepper

Serves 4–6

Put the butter in a small saucepan and set over high heat. Cook until it is melted and sizzling. Before the butter burns, add the flour and stir quickly to form a thick paste. Remove from the heat and add a little of the milk, stirring constantly until thick and smooth. Return the pan to medium heat and add the remaining milk, whisking constantly until all the milk is incorporated and the mixture is smooth and thick. Remove from the heat and let cool.

Preheat the oven to 425°F. Remove the stalks from the mushrooms and sit the mushrooms in a small baking dish, gill-side up. Spoon the cheese sauce into the caps and sprinkle the paprika over the top. Cook in the preheated oven for 20 minutes, until the mushrooms are soft and the sauce is golden and bubbling.

While the mushrooms are cooking, slice the fennel bulb as thinly as possible, chop the fronds finely and put them in a bowl with the parsley, oil, and lemon juice. Toss to combine, season to taste, and serve with the warm mushrooms.

baked mushrooms
with Manchego béchamel

Modern Spanish tapas bars are very popular just now. Hopefully it's not just a passing trend and that they are here to stay, as tapas dishes are shared comfort food at its very best. Mushrooms really are nature's cups just waiting to be filled. Look for ones that will be two to three small mouthfuls when cooked—big cremini mushrooms or smaller portobello mushrooms are both ideal. These are very rich, so a crisp fennel salad is the perfect accompaniment.

crispy oven wedges
with homemade pesto sauce

When was the last time you stirred some freshly made pesto into a big bowl of hot spaghetti? It's an aromatic and heady experience. Food manufacturers like us to believe that pesto keeps in a jar or plastic tub in the fridge, but in fact it soon oxidizes, turning bitter, brown, and oily, and quickly becomes a lesser version of its glorious former self. This vibrant pesto made with handfuls of garden-fresh basil and parsley will knock your socks off and surpass anything you can buy in supermarkets.

2 large floury potatoes, cut into thick wedges

2 tablespoons light olive oil

pesto sauce

2 handfuls of basil leaves

1 handful of flatleaf parsley leaves

1 garlic clove, chopped

1 tablespoon freshly squeezed lemon juice

⅓ cup pine nuts, lightly toasted

¼ cup extra virgin olive oil

½ cup finely grated Parmesan cheese

Serves 4

To make the pesto, put the herbs, garlic, lemon juice, and pine nuts in a food processor and process until finely chopped. With the motor running, add the oil in a steady stream until it is all incorporated. Transfer the mixture to a bowl, stir in the Parmesan, and cover until ready to serve.

Bring a large saucepan of water to a boil and add the potatoes. Boil for 5 minutes, then drain and let cool completely.

Preheat the oven to 425°F. Pour the oil into a roasting pan and put it in the oven for 5 minutes to heat up. Arrange the potato wedges in the pan in a single layer. Cook in the preheated oven for about 15 minutes, turning in the middle of the cooking time, until crisp and golden all over. Transfer to a plate and serve with the pesto on the side for dipping.

Parmesan and bacon pancakes with chive butter

Served warm from the pan, this combination of smoky bacon pancakes and chive butter makes a lovely fireside treat on a chilly day.

1 tablespoon vegetable oil, plus extra for brushing

3 slices of bacon, snipped into small pieces, or 3 oz. pancetta, cubed

¾ cup self-rising flour

1 oz. Parmesan cheese, grated

a pinch of sea salt

1 egg, beaten

scant ⅔ cup full-fat milk

freshly ground black pepper

chive butter

½ stick butter, at room temperature

2–3 tablespoons freshly snipped chives

freshly ground black pepper

Makes about 20 small pancakes

To make the chive butter, put the butter in a bowl and beat in the chives. Season to taste with pepper. Spoon the mixture into a ramekin or small serving bowl, cover and chill until ready to serve.

Put the flour, cheese, and salt in a large bowl and season well with pepper. Make a well in the center. Add the egg and half the milk and gradually work in the flour to make a smooth batter. Beat in the remaining milk to make a smooth batter.

Heat the oil in a large, non-stick skillet and fry the bacon for about 3 minutes, until crispy. Remove the bacon from the pan and drain off any grease. Wipe the pan with paper towels and leave set over low heat.

Drop tablespoonfuls of batter into the pan, sprinkle a little bacon on top and cook for 1–2 minutes, until bubbles appear on the surface. Flip the pancakes over and cook for a further 30 seconds–1 minute, until they are golden. Keep warm while you cook the remaining mixture. Serve warm with the chive butter for spreading.

mini croque-monsieurs

Crisp croque-monsieur sandwiches, oozing with melting Gruyère cheese and ham, are a favorite in French cafés. These miniature versions are the perfect hot savory to serve at teatime. They're very simple to make and you can even prepare them ahead of time and toast when you are ready to serve.

Cut 24 thin slices of baguette, each about about ¼ inch thick. Spread half of the slices with mustard, then top with half the cheese and put a piece of prosciutto on top. Top with the remaining slices of bread.

Preheat the broiler to high. Butter the sandwiches on both sides, then arrange them on the broiler pan. Grill until golden, then turn over and grill until just golden on the other side. Sprinkle with the remaining cheese and grill for 1 minute, or until the cheese is melted and bubbling. Sprinkle with parsley, grind over some black pepper, and serve immediately.

1 baguette

2 teaspoons Dijon mustard

4 oz. Gruyère cheese, grated

4 oz. prosciutto or other ham

butter, at room temperature

chopped flatleaf parsley, to garnish

freshly ground black pepper

Makes 12 small sandwiches

smoked trout rarebit

These hearty rarebits provide just the right combination of indulgence and sustenance. Wonderfully comforting, with an oozing, melted topping, they make a warming snack or light lunch.

2 smoked trout fillets, skinned and flaked

4 thick slices of whole-grain bread

7 oz. cheddar or Gruyère cheese, grated

3½ tablespoons dry white wine

1 shallot, finely chopped

freshly ground black pepper

chopped fresh parsley, to serve

Serves 4

Preheat the broiler to high. Toast the bread on one side only, until golden.

Meanwhile, put the cheese and wine in a saucepan and set over low heat. Gently heat, stirring constantly, until the cheese has melted.

When the bread is golden on one side, turn the slices over and arrange a quarter of the smoked trout on each. Spoon some melted cheese mixture over the top and scatter with some chopped shallot. Season with a little black pepper and return the toasts to the hot broiler. Grill until golden and bubbling. Sprinkle with parsley and serve immediately.

fluffy potato pancakes with smoked salmon

These blini-style pancakes are made with mashed potatoes rather than flour: the result is light and particularly delicious with salty salmon and cool crème fraîche.

1 lb. floury potatoes, peeled and halved

⅔ cup crème fraîche or sour cream

3 eggs, separated

4 tablespoons freshly snipped chives

4 tablespoons unsalted butter

salt and freshly ground black pepper

to serve

1 lb. sliced smoked salmon

1 cup crème fraîche or sour cream

2 tablespoons freshly snipped chives

4 blini pans or 1 large non-stick skillet and 4 ring molds

Serves 4

Put the potatoes in a large saucepan of water, bring to a boil, and cook until tender. Drain, return to the pan, and mash until soft. Beat in the cream and egg yolks. Season well and mix in the chives. Whisk the egg whites until stiff and fold them into the potato mixture.

Heat four blini pans and add ½ tablespoon butter to each*. When the butter is foaming, spoon about 4 tablespoons of the mixture into each pan. Cook until browning and set, then flip over and cook for 1 minute more. Repeat with the remaining butter and potato mixture. Serve the pancakes topped with salmon, crème fraîche, and some chives.

*If using a non-stick skillet and 4 ring molds, drop 4 tablespoons of the mixture into each mold. Cook as above and repeat until all the mixture has been used.

smoked salmon and chive soufflé omelet

⅔ cup full-fat milk

1 small white onion, sliced

1 small carrot, sliced

1 clove

1 fresh or dried bay leaf

9 oz. sliced smoked salmon

6 tablespoons butter

1 tablespoon all-purpose flour

3 large eggs, separated

6 tablespoons sour cream

4 tablespoons freshly snipped chives

2 tablespoons freshly chopped parsley

2 tablespoons freshly grated Parmesan cheese

salt and freshly ground black pepper

Serves 2–4

This light-as-air omelet is a perfect brunch, lunch, or dinner dish and makes an interesting change from the usual scrambled eggs with smoked salmon.

Put the milk in a saucepan with the onion, carrot, clove, and bay leaf. Heat until almost boiling, then turn off the heat and let stand for 10 minutes. Add half the smoked salmon and simmer for 5 minutes until it is opaque. Remove the fish to a plate and flake it with a fork. Strain and reserve the milk.

Melt half the butter in a small saucepan and stir in the flour. Gradually whisk in the reserved milk and bring the mixture to a boil, stirring all the time until a thickened sauce. Remove from the heat.

Put the egg yolks and half the sour cream in a bowl, beat well, then stir into the sauce. Carefully stir in the cooked smoked salmon, chives, and parsley and season to taste. Whisk the egg whites in a bowl until stiff and fold into the sauce.

Preheat the oven to 400°F. Melt the remaining butter in a skillet with a heatproof handle and pour in the salmon mixture. Cook over a medium heat until just beginning to set, then scatter over the remaining salmon and spoon over the remaining sour cream. Carefully flip one half of the omelet over to cover the salmon. Scatter with Parmesan and finish off in the preheated oven for 5 minutes. Serve immediately, straight from the pan.

dinner dishes

sticky pork tenderloin with a pecorino crust, mustard mash, and balsamic onions

Tender pork with a golden, rosemary-flecked cheese crust, fluffy mustard-speckled mashed potatoes and sticky, savory-sweet onions add up to cloud nine dining.

2 x 14-oz. pieces of whole pork tenderloin

3 tablespoons extra virgin olive oil

1½ cups finely grated pecorino cheese

a small bunch of rosemary, chopped

sea salt and freshly ground black pepper

mustard mash

2 lbs. floury potatoes, peeled and cubed

1–2 tablespoons whole-grain mustard (to taste)

2 garlic cloves, crushed

3–4 tablespoons full-fat milk

4–5 tablespoons extra virgin olive oil

balsamic onions

2 tablespoons extra virgin olive oil

6 red onions, peeled and thinly sliced

⅓ cup balsamic vinegar

Serves 4

Preheat the oven to 400°F.

Brush the pork fillets with 1 tablespoon of the olive oil. Mix the pecorino and rosemary together and spread over a sheet of baking parchment. Roll the pork fillets in the mixture, pressing down well so they are evenly coated. Put them in a roasting pan and drizzle with the remaining oil. Roast in the preheated oven for 30 minutes, or until the pork is cooked through and the crusts are golden. Leave to rest in a warm place.

To make the mash, boil the potatoes in a large saucepan of salted water until soft. Drain, return to the warm pan, and mash. Beat in the mustard, garlic, milk, and olive oil. Cover and keep warm.

To make the onions, heat the olive oil in a skillet and add the onions. Cook for 3–4 minutes, until light golden and starting to soften. Add the balsamic vinegar and 3 tablespoons water. Cook slowly for about 10 minutes, or until the onions are soft and sticky, then season to taste. Slice the pork and serve with mash and balsamic onions.

poulet sauté au vinaigre

Typically, this traditional French dish is thickened and enriched with butter but this recipe uses extra virgin olive oil instead. The one thing that definitely isn't up for negotiation is the use of excellent-quality red wine vinegar. Cheap vinegar is far too astringent for this dish and will produce a harsh and unpleasant sauce—a far cry from the mouth-watering result you should get.

⅓ cup extra virgin olive oil

a 4–5 lb. chicken, cut into 8 pieces

1 lb. very ripe cherry tomatoes (or 14-oz can cherry tomatoes in juice, drained before using)

2 garlic cloves, crushed

¾ cup very good-quality red wine vinegar

1¼ cups chicken stock

a small bunch of flatleaf parsley, chopped

sea salt and freshly ground black pepper

mixed salad greens, to serve

Serves 4–6

Heat 3 tablespoons of the olive oil in a large skillet. Season the chicken all over and cook for 3–4 minutes on each side, or until golden. Add the tomatoes and garlic to the pan. Cook for 10–15 minutes, squashing the tomatoes down with the back of a spoon, until they are thick and sticky and have lost all their moisture.

Pour in the vinegar and leave it to bubble for 10–15 minutes, until the liquid has almost evaporated. Pour in the stock, and cook for a further 15 minutes or so, until the liquid has reduced by half. Stir in the remaining olive oil and the parsley. Spoon onto serving plates and add a generous handful of mixed salad greens to serve.

Put 3 cups water in a large saucepan. Set over high heat, cover with a lid, and heat until simmering. Pour the polenta into the pan of simmering water and beat out any lumps. Reduce the heat to low and let it bubble for 30–40 minutes. (If you are using quick-cook polenta, cook according to the package instructions.)

To make the gravy, heat the olive oil in a skillet and cook the onions and rosemary over medium heat, stirring constantly. When the onions are just starting to soften, reduce the heat, cover, and leave to soften slowly in their own juices. After about 10–15 minutes, stir in the flour and cook for about 1 minute until it is no longer pale. Add the red currant jelly, wine, and stock and bring to a boil. Leave to bubble away gently for 15 minutes while you cook the sausages.

Preheat the broiler to high. Put the sausages on a broiler pan lined with foil and cook for about 15 minutes, turning halfway through, until well browned and cooked through.

Beat the butter and Parmesan into the polenta and season well. Beat the butter into the gravy and season to taste. Spoon the polenta into dishes, top with sausages, and pour over the hot gravy to serve.

herby sausages on polenta with red onion and red currant gravy

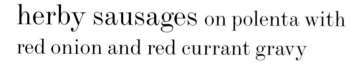

This is an Italian take on sausage and mash with a bit of British red currant jelly thrown in because it makes onion gravy lovely and sticky. If you've tried polenta before and weren't blown away, try it again now: the secret is plenty of butter, cheese, and seasoning.

12 good-quality sausages with herbs

sea salt and freshly ground black pepper

red onion and red currant gravy

2 tablespoons extra virgin olive oil

2 red onions, thinly sliced

2 rosemary sprigs, broken up

2 teaspoons all-purpose flour

2 tablespoons red currant jelly

1¼ cups red wine

1¼ cups beef stock

2 tablespoons butter

polenta

1 cup traditional or quick-cook polenta

3½ tablespoons butter

¾ cup freshly grated Parmesan cheese

Serves 4

polenta baked with Italian sausage and cheese

A real winter warmer to eat by a roaring fire. This is sublime comfort food, loaded with sausage and strings of melting cheese. If you can't find Italian sausages, choose those with the highest meat content and bags of flavor. Spicy Spanish chorizo would also be great in this dish.

2 cups traditional or quick-cook polenta

1 lb. fresh Italian sausages (or good, strongly flavored butcher's sausages)

1 tablespoon olive oil

1 red onion, finely chopped

⅔ cup vegetable or meat stock

3 tablespoons chopped rosemary and sage, mixed

12 oz. Taleggio cheese, chopped or grated

1½ cups grated Parmesan cheese

a few pieces of butter

sea salt and freshly ground black pepper

a shallow ovenproof dish, buttered

Serves 6

To make the polenta, bring 4 cups salted water to a boil, then slowly sprinkle in the polenta through your fingers, whisking all the time to prevent lumps. Cook, stirring with a wooden spoon, for 45 minutes over low heat. Transfer from the pan to a wooden board and shape into a mound. Let cool and set. (If you are using quick-cook polenta, cook according to the package instructions.)

Slice the sausages very thickly. Heat the olive oil in a skillet, add the sausages, and sauté until browned on all sides. Add the onion and cook for 5 minutes until softening. Add the stock and half the chopped herbs, salt, and pepper.

Preheat the oven to 350°F.

Cut the polenta into ½-inch slices. Arrange a layer of polenta in the prepared dish. Add half the sausage mixture, half the Taleggio, and half the Parmesan, in layers. Cover with another layer of polenta, add layers of the remaining sausage mixture, Taleggio, and Parmesan and dot with a few pieces of butter. Sprinkle with the remaining herbs. Bake in the preheated oven for 40 minutes until brown and bubbling. Serve warm.

meatballs in spicy red sauce

The combination of tomato, orange, and chile gives this dish a Spanish flavor. Any part of this dish—sauce and/or meatballs—can be made a day ahead; in fact, it's better that way. Serve with roasted or sautéed potatoes.

meatballs

1 cup fresh bread crumbs

3 tablespoons milk

1 small white onion

a handful of flatleaf parsley leaves

2 garlic cloves

1 lb. 12 oz. ground beef or pork or a mixture

1½ teaspoons fine sea salt

1 teaspoon dried oregano

1 teaspoon ground cumin

½ teaspoon Spanish smoked paprika (pimentón)

1 egg, beaten

3 tablespoons extra virgin olive oil

spicy red sauce

2 red bell peppers

2 tablespoons extra virgin olive oil, plus extra for rubbing

several sprigs of thyme

1 fresh or dried bay leaf

1 white onion, grated

6 garlic cloves, crushed

¼ teaspoon cayenne pepper (optional)

5 tablespoons red wine

½ an orange

4 cups passata (sieved tomatoes)

sea salt and freshly ground black pepper

kitchen twine

a large ovenproof dish

Makes about 25 meatballs

Preheat the oven to 425°F.

To make the spicy red sauce, rub the bell peppers with olive oil, then put them on a sheet of foil on a baking sheet (make the foil large enough to fold over and enclose the peppers after roasting.) Roast in the preheated oven for about 30–40 minutes, until tender and charred. Remove from the oven, enclose in the foil, and set aside. When cool enough to handle, remove the skins and seeds, chop the flesh coarsely and set aside. Lower the oven temperature to 400°F.

Meanwhile, tie up the thyme and bay leaf with kitchen twine. Heat 2 tablespoons of the oil in a heavy-based skillet. Add the onion and a pinch of salt and cook until soft, 2–3 minutes. Add the garlic and cayenne, if using, and cook, stirring, for 1 minute. Stir in the wine and squeeze in the orange juice (reserve the rest of the orange) and cook for 30 seconds. Add the passata, a good pinch of salt, the bunch of herbs, and the reserved orange. Simmer gently for about 20–30 minutes, until thick. Season to taste. Stir in the bell peppers, remove the herbs and orange and transfer to a baking dish large enough to hold the meatballs in a single layer. This can be done a day ahead.

To make the meatballs, put the bread crumbs, milk, onion, parsley, garlic, ground meat, salt, oregano, cumin, paprika, and beaten egg in a large bowl. Mix well (your hands are best). Shape spoonfuls of the meat mixture into golf ball-size balls and set on a baking sheet.

To cook, heat the 3 tablespoons of the oil in a large, heavy-based skillet. Working in batches, cook the meatballs for about 5 minutes per batch, until browned evenly. Using a slotted spoon, transfer the browned meatballs to the sauce in the baking dish. When all the meatballs are browned, gently spoon some sauce over each one, then cover the baking dish with foil and bake in the preheated oven for 20 minutes. Serve hot with sautéed potatoes.

quick Thai chicken curry

You can add any vegetables to this basic curry recipe, such as mushrooms, French beans, fresh spinach, bamboo shoots, zucchini, or carrot—it's perfect for using up odds and ends.

1¾ cups coconut milk

3 tablespoons Thai green curry paste

1 tablespoon vegetable oil

1 chicken breast (about 14 oz.), cut into bite-size pieces

½ teaspoon kaffir lime leaf purée

1 teaspoon Thai fish sauce

6 oz. mixed fresh vegetables

a handful of basil leaves

jasmine rice

1 cup Thai jasmine rice

2 tablespoons unsalted butter

a pinch of fine sea salt

a wok (optional)

Serves 2

To make the jasmine rice, put the rice in a large saucepan with a tight-fitting lid. Add 1½ cups cold water, the butter, and salt. Bring to a boil then reduce the heat to a simmer. Cover and cook for about 20 minutes or until the rice has absorbed all the liquid (add a little more water if the rice is not yet tender.)

Meanwhile, pour the coconut milk into a separate saucepan and gently bring it to near boiling point. Remove the pan from the heat and stir in the Thai curry paste. Set aside.

Pour the oil into a wok or large skillet and stir-fry the chicken pieces over high heat for about 2 minutes, until golden. Pour the coconut milk mixture over the fried chicken pieces and add the kaffir lime leaf purée and fish sauce. Add the vegetables, stir, and simmer gently for about 12 minutes, or until everything is cooked through.

Remove the rice from the heat and let it sit for 5 minutes. Fluff it up with a fork just before serving. Scatter the basil over the curry and serve with a small bowl of jasmine rice on the side.

chicken jalfrezi

This versatile curry recipe can also be made with beef, lamb, shrimp, or fish instead of chicken. If using fish, choose a firm white variety such as swordfish, marlin, monkfish, or kingfish.

¼ cup vegetable oil

1½ large yellow onions, sliced

2 garlic cloves, chopped

a 2-inch piece of fresh ginger, peeled and chopped or grated

2 red or green chiles, chopped

1 teaspoon ground turmeric

2 cardamom pods, lightly crushed

2 teaspoons mild curry powder

1 teaspoon ground coriander

1 teaspoon ground cumin

4 lbs. chicken, cut into chunks

6 cups canned chopped tomatoes

freshly squeezed juice of 2 limes and 1 lemon

a large handful of cilantro, chopped, to serve

sea salt and freshly ground black pepper

Serves 6

Heat the oil in a large saucepan. Add the onion, garlic, and chiles and cook until soft, making sure they do not brown. Add the turmeric, cardamom, curry powder, ground coriander, and cumin and cook for 2 minutes. Add the chicken, sprinkle with salt and pepper and stir until coated with the spices. Cook for 5 minutes until the chicken is opaque on the outside. Add the tomatoes, mix well, cover with a lid, and simmer for 30 minutes, stirring from time to time. Add the lime and lemon juices, simmer for 3 minutes and sprinkle with chopped cilantro to serve.

¼ cup olive oil

3 shallots, finely chopped

2 garlic cloves, chopped

6 oz. portobello mushrooms, sliced

3½ lbs. beef tenderloin, trimmed

1 lb. ready-made puff or shortcrust pastry, thawed if frozen

2 eggs, beaten

sea salt and freshly ground black pepper

mustard sauce

2 tablespoons smooth Dijon mustard

2 tablespoons whole-grain mustard

½ cup white wine

1¾ cups heavy cream

reserved juices from roasting the beef tenderloin

Serves 8

beef en croûte
with mustard sauce

This is a French classic that's perfect for smart dinners. The sauce is delicious but also very rich—a little goes a long way.

Put 2 tablespoons of the oil into a skillet and set over low heat. Add the shallots, garlic, and mushrooms and gently sauté for about 15 minutes, stirring frequently, until soft but not browned and all the liquid has evaporated. Season with salt and pepper, let cool, then cover and chill.

Preheat the oven to 425°F.

Put 1 tablespoon of the remaining oil into a roasting pan and put it in the preheated oven to heat for 5 minutes.

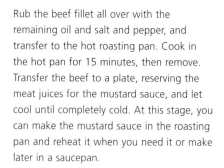

Rub the beef fillet all over with the remaining oil and salt and pepper, and transfer to the hot roasting pan. Cook in the hot pan for 15 minutes, then remove. Transfer the beef to a plate, reserving the meat juices for the mustard sauce, and let cool until completely cold. At this stage, you can make the mustard sauce in the roasting pan and reheat it when you need it or make later in a saucepan.

To make the mustard sauce, add the mustards, white wine, and heavy cream to the roasting pan with the meat juices. Bring to a boil, then simmer for 5 minutes. Remove from the heat, cover, and set aside until ready to serve.

Roll out the pastry to a rectangle large enough to wrap around the beef. Brush lightly with a little of the beaten egg. Spoon the mushroom mixture evenly over the pastry, leaving a 2 inch border around the outside. Put the cold beef in the middle of the pastry, on top of the mushrooms, and either roll the pastry around the tenderloin or wrap, as if covering a package. Try not to have too much pastry at the ends, and trim to avoid areas of double pastry. Turn the parcel so that the seam is underneath and transfer to a lightly oiled baking sheet. Brush all over with the remaining beaten egg and chill for 2 hours.

Preheat the oven to 400°F. Cook on the middle shelf of the preheated oven for 20 minutes. Reduce the oven temperature to 350°F and continue cooking for 15 minutes for rare, 35 minutes for medium, and 50 minutes for well done. If you are cooking to well done, you may need to reduce the oven temperature further to prevent the pastry from burning while the beef cooks through.

When ready to serve, reheat the mustard sauce if necessary, plate slices of the beef, and pour a little of the sauce around the outside. Serve immediately with sautéed green beans on the side, if liked.

pan-fried tuna steaks with warm vincotto-dressed lentils

The combination of earthy lentils and sweet, rich vincotto (grape must) is stunning. This recipe works well with good quality balsamic vinegar too, but vincotto definitely has the edge.

1½ cups Puy or beluga lentils

3 tablespoons olive oil

1 white onion

4 oz. pancetta lardons

2 tablespoons vincotto or good quality balsamic vinegar

4 fresh tuna steaks

sea salt and freshly ground black pepper

freshly squeezed juice of ½ a lemon

Serves 4

Cook the lentils according to the package instructions. Meanwhile, heat 2 tablespoons of the olive oil in a skillet and gently sauté the onion for a few minutes, until softened but not colored. Add the pancetta and cook until crisp. Drain the lentils and add them to the pan. Stir in the vincotto and keep warm.

Brush the tuna with the remaining olive oil and season well. Heat a ridged stovetop grill pan or non-stick skillet. Cook the tuna steaks for 1–2 minutes on each side, depending on how thick they are. (Take care not to overcook the fish as it will be unpleasantly tough and chewy.) Squeeze a little lemon juice over the fish and serve with the warm lentils.

chunky fish stew with cheese toasts

1 small onion, finely chopped

2 garlic cloves, 1 crushed; 1 peeled and halved

a pinch of dried thyme

1 small fennel bulb, hard core removed and finely chopped

1 tablespoon olive oil

2 oz. Noilly Prat, dry Martini, or dry white wine

2 cups passata (sieved tomatoes)

1 pinch of saffron threads

freshly squeezed juice and finely grated peel of 1 orange

8 oz. skinless cod fillet, cut into large chunks

sea salt and freshly ground black pepper

4 thin slices of baguette

¼ cup finely grated Emmental or Gruyère cheese

Serves 2

If you have ever tasted the classic French fish soup bouillabaisse and enjoyed the flavor, then this is a good cheat's version. The combination of saffron, orange, and fennel gives the stew its distinctive flavor.

Put the olive oil in a large saucepan and set over low heat. Add the chopped onion, crushed garlic, thyme, and fennel and gently sauté, stirring occassionally, for about 6–8 minutes or until soft but not browned. Add the Noilly Prat and let bubble, uncovered, until the liquid has reduced to almost nothing.

Add the passata, saffron, orange juice, and grated peel and 1 scant cup cold water. Increase the heat to medium and cook for 10 minutes. Add the fish and cook gently for 2 minutes, then taste to taste.

Meanwhile, preheat the broiler to high. Toast the baguette slices under the hot broiler until lightly golden on both sides. Rub the halved garlic over each slice and sprinkle with the grated cheese.

Ladle the stew into warmed serving bowls. Sit two cheese-topped toasts on top and serve immediately.

herb and nut crusted salmon fillets

Serve this deliciously easy yet impressive fish dish with a pile of buttery leeks and creamy mashed potatoes flavored with a little whole-grain mustard.

1 tablespoon mixed red, green, and white dry peppercorns, crushed

4 salmon fillets (about 6 oz. each), skin on

5 cups fresh whole-wheat bread crumbs

⅔ cup shelled walnuts, chopped

½ cup mixed chopped green herbs

finely grated peel of 1 orange

freshly grated nutmeg, to taste

1 stick butter, melted

1 egg yolk, beaten

salt and freshly ground black pepper

tartare sauce

⅔ cup real mayonnaise

1 tablespoon chopped capers

1 tablespoon chopped gherkins

1 tablespoon chopped parsley

1 shallot, finely chopped

1 teaspoon freshly squeezed lemon juice

sea salt and freshly ground black pepper

Serves 4

Rub the crushed peppercorns all over the flesh side of the salmon fillets. Put them in a baking dish, skin-side up, cover, and set aside.

Mix the bread crumbs with the walnuts, herbs, and grated orange peel and add ground nutmeg to taste. Set a skillet over high heat, add the butter and, when foaming, stir in the bread crumb mixture. Cook until the butter is absorbed and the bread crumbs are beginning to brown. Season well and set aside.

Preheat the oven to 400°F. Brush the salmon skin with egg yolk and press on the bread crumbs. Bake in the preheated oven for 15–20 minutes, until the fish is opaque and the bread crumbs crisp.

To make the tartare sauce, mix all the ingredients together in a small bowl and serve as a spooning sauce with the fish.

roast onion and celeriac ravioli
with warm walnut pesto

Walnuts and celeriac make a magical combination, especially when the celeriac is roasted with onion and tucked inside ravioli, as it is here. However, if time is short, try this lovely pesto tossed through pasta tubes such as rigatoni or penne.

sea salt and freshly ground black pepper

semolina, to dust

pasta

3 cups Italian "00" flour

4 eggs, beaten

filling

1 celeriac, peeled and cubed

1 large white onion, finely chopped

1 garlic clove, peeled and crushed

1 teaspoon thyme leaves

2 tablespoons clear honey

3 tablespoons extra virgin olive oil

walnut pesto

⅔ cups shelled walnut pieces

2 garlic cloves, peeled and crushed

3 tablespoons finely chopped rosemary needles

½ cup finely grated pecorino or Parmesan cheese

4 tablespoons walnut oil

Serves 4

To make the pasta, sift the flour into a bowl or food processor. Add the eggs and bring the mixture together to make a soft but not sticky dough. Turn out on to a lightly floured surface and knead for 4–5 minutes, until smooth. Wrap in plastic wrap and refrigerate for at least 30 minutes.

Preheat the oven to 400°F.

To make the filling, put the celeriac, onion, garlic, and thyme in a roasting pan. Drizzle with the honey and olive oil, season well, and toss to coat in the mixture. Roast in the preheated oven for about 25 minutes, or until the celeriac is soft and golden. Leave to cool slightly, then mash coarsely.

To make the pesto, chop the walnuts, garlic, and rosemary very finely in a food processor or by hand. Stir in the pecorino and walnut oil. Season to taste.

Roll out the chilled pasta dough to a thickness of ¹⁄₁₆ inch using a pasta machine or a rolling pin. Cut the pasta into two long pieces of equal size. Place teaspoonfuls of the filling at even intervals across one half of the pasta. Brush around the filling with a little water and cover with the second sheet. Press lightly around the filling to seal, then cut into squares using a sharp knife or pastry wheel. Lay out the ravioli on baking parchment lightly dusted with semolina.

Bring a large saucepan of salted water to a boil and drop in the ravioli. Cook for 2–3 minutes, until the pasta rises to the surface and is soft but still retains a little bite. Drain and toss immediately with the walnut pesto. Serve at once.

pasta with broccoli, ricotta, and walnuts

The light texture and creamy flavor of ricotta cheese makes the perfect backdrop to walnuts and broccoli in this deliciously simple and quick pasta dish.

⅔ cup shelled walnut halves

1 head of broccoli, about about 1 lb.

3 tablespoons light olive oil

3 garlic cloves, thinly sliced

1 handful of flatleaf parsley, chopped

finely grated peel and freshly squeezed juice of 1 lemon

7 oz. fresh ricotta cheese

14 oz. spaghetti

sea salt and freshly ground black pepper

Serves 4

Preheat the oven to 350°F.

Spread the walnuts out on a baking sheet and roast in the preheated oven for about 8 minutes, shaking the tray occasionally, until they start to brown.

To prepare the broccoli, trim off the gnarly part, about 1 inch from the stem end, and discard. Thinly slice the stem until you reach the point where it starts to branch into florets. Slice off the individual florets. Heat the oil in a skillet, add the stems and cook for about 2–3 minutes, turning often, then add the florets and cook for about 5 minutes, until the broccoli has softened. Add the garlic, parsley, grated lemon peel, and walnuts and cook for 5 minutes, stirring often. Reduce the heat to medium and stir in the ricotta and lemon juice. Season well and leave in the pan to keep warm.

Cook the spaghetti according to the package instructions. Drain and return to the warm pan with the sauce. Stir gently to combine and serve immediately.

mushroom and thyme ragù with hand-torn pasta

2 tablespoons light olive oil

2 tablespoons butter

1 white onion, chopped

2 garlic cloves, chopped

3 portobello mushrooms, caps removed and cut into 1-inch pieces

6 oz. button mushrooms

4 oz. fresh shiitake mushrooms, quartered

3 thyme sprigs

1 cup red wine

1 cinnamon stick

1 cup vegetable or beef stock

14 oz. fresh lasagne sheets, cut or torn into thick strips

sea salt and freshly ground black pepper

freshly grated Parmesan cheese, to serve

Serves 4

Heat the oil and butter in a heavy-based saucepan set over medium heat. Add the onion and garlic and cook for 4–5 minutes, until the onions have softened. Increase the heat to high, add the mushrooms, and thyme and cook for a further 8–10 minutes, stirring often, until the mushrooms darken and soften.

Add the red wine and cinnamon to the pan and boil rapidly for 5 minutes. Pour in the stock and season well. Reduce the heat to low and let the mixture gently simmer, uncovered, for 35–40 minutes.

Cook the pasta in a saucepan of salted boiling water for 2–3 minutes, until it rises to the surface. Drain well and place in serving bowls. Spoon the mushroom ragù over the top, sprinkle with Parmesan, and serve immediately.

This recipe calls for a mixture of mushrooms—portobello, button, and shiitake have been used here but do look out for other exotic varieties, many of which can now be bought year-round. Cremini and oyster mushrooms would also work well with the rich, comforting flavors of fresh thyme, red wine, and cinnamon.

spaghetti with butternut squash, sage, and pecorino

¼ cup light olive oil

14 oz. butternut squash, peeled, seeded, and sliced into thin wedges

2 garlic cloves, chopped

10–12 small sage leaves

14 oz. spaghetti

1 handful of flatleaf parsley, chopped

½ cup grated pecorino or Parmesan cheese

sea salt and freshly ground black pepper

Serves 4

Put the oil in a skillet and set over high heat. Add the squash and cook for 5–6 minutes, turning often, until golden but not breaking up. Add the garlic and sage to the pan and cook for 2–3 minutes. Remove from the heat and set aside to allow the flavors to develop.

Cook the pasta according to the package instructions. Drain well and return it to the warm pan with the squash mixture. Add the parsley and half of the pecorino. Season well and toss gently to combine. Sprinkle the remaining pecorino over the top and serve immediately.

This tasty pasta is inspired by the classic Italian dish of pumpkin-filled ravioli with sage butter, except this is an inside-out version and therefore much easier to make! Butternut squash is used here, but you could also use pumpkin.

Swiss chard, feta cheese, and egg pie

The pastry here is based on the Turkish version of pizza dough (pide), which is often filled or topped with the freshest of vegetables such as tomatoes, spinach or chard, or tangy feta cheese and sometimes with an egg or two cracked on top before being baked. It's very easy to see where the inspiration for this delicious open pie came from!

3 tablespoons olive oil

2 garlic cloves, sliced

1 red onion, thinly sliced

1 lb. Swiss chard, chopped

4 eggs

7 oz. feta cheese, crumbled

sea salt and freshly ground black pepper

pastry

2 cups all-purpose flour

1 stick plus 2 tablespoons unsalted butter, cut into cubes

2 egg yolks

2–3 tablespoons ice water

Serves 6

To make the pastry, put the flour and butter in the bowl of a food processor and put the bowl in the freezer for 10 minutes. Pulse the ingredients a few times until just combined. With the motor of the food processor running, add the egg yolks and just enough ice water so that the mixture is on the verge of coming together. Do not overbeat, as this will make the pastry tough. Remove the dough from the bowl and use lightly floured hands to quickly form it into a ball. Wrap in plastic wrap and let rest in the fridge for 30 minutes.

Put 2 tablespoons of the oil in a skillet and set over high heat. Add the onion and garlic and cook for 2 minutes, until it softens and just flavors the oil. Add the Swiss chard to the pan and cook for about 5 minutes, stirring often, until it wilts and softens. Season well, leave in the pan, and set aside to cool.

Preheat the oven to 425°F.

Roll the pastry dough out on lightly floured baking parchment to form a circle about 14 inches in diameter, trimming away any uneven bits. Roll the edge over to form a ½-inch border, then roll over again. Transfer the pastry to a baking sheet. Spoon the Swiss chard mixture over the top. Put the eggs in a bowl and prick the yolks with a fork. Pour them over the Swiss chard then scatter the feta over the top. Drizzle the remaining oil over the pie and cook in the preheated oven for about 20 minutes, until the pastry is golden and the top of the pie is just starting to turn brown. Let cool for 10 minutes before cutting into slices to serve.

egg, bacon, and spinach pie

Fall is a great time for pies. The weather is often fickle and you have the option of serving it with boiled and buttered potatoes or salad greens if the days are still mild. Any leftovers will keep in the fridge for a few days so you can enjoy them as late dinner.

1lb. fresh spinach

1 tablespoon butter

3 slices of rindless bacon, cut into thin strips

1 white onion, finely chopped

6 eggs, lightly beaten

½ cup finely grated Parmesan cheese

1 egg, lightly beaten with 1 tablespoon cold water

shortcrust pastry

2 cups all-purpose flour

1 stick plus 2 tablespoons butter, cut into small cubes

1 egg yolk

a loose-based tart pan, 8 inches diameter, lightly greased

Serves 6

Put the flour and butter into the bowl of a food processor and put the bowl into the freezer for 15 minutes. Lightly beat the egg yolk with 2 tablespoons water and refrigerate for 15 minutes. Process the butter and flour until the mixture looks like ground almonds, then add the egg yolk mixture and process for just a few seconds to combine. Tip the mixture into a bowl and use your hands to bring the dough together to form one large ball. It should be a bit crumbly. Wrap in plastic wrap and refrigerate for 30 minutes.

Preheat the oven to 350°F.

Wash the spinach well, leaving some of the water on the leaves. Put it in a large non-stick skillet and set over high heat. Cook for 2 minutes, until wilted. Transfer to a colander and drain well. When cool enough to handle, use your hands to squeeze out as much water as possible from the spinach and place it in a large bowl.

Heat the butter in the skillet set over high heat. When sizzling, add the bacon and onion and cook for 5 minutes until golden. Spoon the mixture into the bowl with the spinach. Add the eggs and Parmesan and season well. Stir to combine.

Put the prepared tart pan on a baking sheet. Cut two-thirds from the dough and roll it out between two layers of baking parchment. Line the bottom of the tart pan with the pastry. Spoon the spinach mixture on top of the pastry base. Roll the remaining pastry out into a circle slightly larger than the tart pan. Place this on top of the pie, allowing any excess pastry to hang over the edge and gently press down around the edges to seal. Brush with the egg and water mixture and bake in the preheated oven for 1 hour, until golden.

Let the pie cool for about 10–15 minutes before cutting into wedges. Serve with boiled new potatoes or salad greens, if liked.

chicken, leek, and tarragon pot pie

When fall really sets in it is good to know you can rely on one shining beacon of fresh-grown produce: the leek. While most other vegetables are waiting for spring to make it to the dinner table again, summer-planted leeks will be ready to enjoy long after the summer has gone. Do look out for anise-flavored fresh tarragon as it's particularly good with chicken and cream and works a treat here. The pastry recipe isn't as intimidating as it looks so do try it at least once before resorting to frozen ready-made pie dough.

3 tablespoons butter

1½ lbs. chicken thigh fillets, cut into bite-size pieces

4 leeks (white parts only), thickly sliced

3 tablespoons all-purpose flour

1 cup chicken stock

½ cup light cream

2 tablespoons finely chopped tarragon

2 tablespoons roughly chopped flatleaf parsley

sea salt and freshly ground black pepper

pie pastry

1½ cups all-purpose flour

2 tablespoons butter

2 tablespoons sour cream

1 egg, lightly beaten

a large, deep pie dish

Serves 4

Put half of the butter in a large skillet and set over high heat. When the butter is sizzling, add the chicken and cook for 2–3 minutes, turning often until browned all over. Transfer to a bowl.

Add the remaining butter to the pan and cook the leeks over medium heat for 2 minutes. Cover with a lid, reduce the heat, and gently cook for 2–3 minutes, until very soft.

Return the chicken to the pan and increase the heat to high. Sprinkle the flour into the pan and cook for 2 minutes, stirring constantly so that the flour thickly coats the chicken and leeks. Gradually add the chicken stock, stirring all the time. Bring to a boil, then stir in the cream, tarragon, and parsley. Season well. Reduce the heat and gently simmer until thickened. Remove from the heat and let cool. Spoon the mixture into the pie dish.

To make the pastry, put the flour, butter, and a pinch of salt in a food processor and process for a few seconds. With the motor running, add the sour cream, half of the beaten egg, and 1–2 tablespoons cold water. Mix until the dough comes together. Roll into a ball, wrap in plastic wrap, and refrigerate for 30 minutes.

Preheat the oven to 350°F. Put the dough between two pieces of baking parchment and roll out to a thickness of ¼ inch, making sure the dough is more than big enough to cover the dish. Fold the dough over the top of the pie, leaving the edges to overhang. Cut several slits in the top of the pie and gently press down around the edges with the tines of a fork to seal. Brush the remaining beaten egg over the top.

Put the pie dish on a baking sheet and cook in the preheated oven for about 30 minutes, until the pastry is golden.

steak and wild mushroom pies

This glorious recipe can be baked as six individual pies or one large pie, as preferred, and can be completely made ahead of time. Make the beef stew in advance, top with the pastry, and refrigerate until ready to put in the oven. Mixed dried wild mushrooms are available in most supermarkets.

2 oz. dried wild mushrooms

6 tablespoons olive oil or beef dripping

1 white onion, finely chopped

3 garlic cloves, chopped

1 large carrot, finely chopped

2 celery ribs, finely chopped

5 oz. cubed pancetta or chopped bacon slices

8 juniper berries, crushed

3 fresh or dried bay leaves

2 tablespoons chopped thyme

2 tablespoons all-purpose flour

2 lbs. stewing beef, trimmed and cut into large cubes

1¼ cups red wine

2 tablespoons red currant jelly

1 lb. ready-rolled puff pastry dough, thawed if frozen

1 egg, beaten

sea salt and freshly ground black pepper

a large casserole dish (optional)

6 individual pie dishes or 1 large pie dish

Serves 6

Put the dried mushrooms in a bowl, just cover with hot water, and let soak for 30 minutes. Meanwhile, heat half the oil in a large casserole dish or saucepan, add the onion, garlic, carrot, and celery and cook for 5–10 minutes until softening. Stir in the pancetta and fry with the vegetables until just beginning to brown. Add the juniper berries, bay leaves, and thyme, sprinkle in the flour, mix well, and set aside.

Heat the remaining olive oil in a large skillet and fry the beef quickly (in batches) on all sides until crusty and brown. Transfer to the casserole dish as you go. When done, deglaze the skillet with the wine, let bubble, then scrape up the sediment from the bottom of the pan. Pour over the meat and vegetables. Drain the mushrooms and add to the casserole dish with ⅔ cup of the soaking water and the red currant jelly. Season well and bring to a boil on the stovetop, then let gently simmer for 1½ hours until the meat is tender. Let cool overnight.

Next day, preheat the the oven to 425°F. Spoon the beef mixture into 6 small pie dishes. Cut out 6 circles of pastry, 1 inch wider than the dishes. Alternatively, use a large pie dish and roll the pastry wider than the dish, as before. Brush the edges of the dishes with egg, sit the dough on top and press over the rim to seal. Brush with more egg, but don't pierce the tops (the steam must be trapped inside). Put the pies on 2 baking sheets and chill for 30 minutes. Bake in the preheated oven for 20–25 minutes (or 45 minutes–1 hour for the large pie) until the pastry is risen and crisp and golden.

goat cheese, leek, and walnut tart

9 oz. ready-made puff pastry dough, thawed if frozen

4 tablespoons butter

4 small leeks, trimmed and sliced

8 oz. goat cheese log with rind, sliced

sea salt and freshly ground black pepper

freshly chopped parsley, to serve

walnut paste

1¼ cups shelled walnut pieces

3 garlic cloves, crushed

6 tablespoons walnut oil

3 tablespoons chopped parsley

an 11-inch diameter dinner plate or similar

Serves 4–6

This light, creamy open tart is easy to make because there is no need to line a pan or bake blind—simply roll out the dough and top it as you would a pizza. Goat cheese and walnuts are a great combination, especially combined here with soft earthy leeks.

Preheat the oven to 400°F.

Roll the pastry out thinly on a lightly floured work surface. Cut out an 11-inch circle using the dinner plate as a template. Set on a baking sheet and chill or freeze for at least 15 minutes.

Melt the butter in a large saucepan and add the leeks, stirring to coat. Add a few tablespoons of water and a teaspoon of salt, and cover with a lid. Steam very gently for at least 20 minutes, until just softening. Remove the lid and cook for a few minutes to evaporate any excess liquid. Let cool.

To make the walnut paste, blend the walnuts and garlic in a food processor with 2 tablespoons water. Mix in the walnut oil and stir in the parsley. Spread this over the pastry, avoiding the rim.

Spoon the leeks into the pastry shell and top with the goat cheese. Drizzle with any remaining walnut paste. Season well and sprinkle with olive oil. Bake in the preheated oven for 20 minutes, until the pastry is golden and the cheese bubbling and brown. Sprinkle with parsley and serve immediately.

potato and Parmesan tart

Real comfort food for a miserable wet weekend! This is a deliciously creamy tart, which makes a casual dinner dish when served with smoked salmon or a few slices of crisply fried bacon.

14-oz. ready-made shortcrust pastry dough, thawed if frozen

2 lbs. starchy white potatoes, such as Desirée, thinly sliced (do not rinse the potatoes as their starch will help to thicken the cream)

4 tablespoons butter, cut into pieces

¼ cup freshly grated Parmesan cheese

4 tablespoons freshly snipped chives

freshly grated nutmeg, to taste

1 egg, beaten

2¼ cups heavy cream

sea salt and freshly ground black pepper

a deep tart pan or dish

foil or baking parchment and baking weights

Serves 4–6

Preheat the oven to 400°F.

Roll out the pastry thinly on a lightly floured work surface. Use the pastry to line the pan or dish, then prick the base all over with a fork. Chill or freeze for 15 minutes.

Line the pastry shell with foil, then fill with baking weights. Set on a baking sheet and bake blind in the preheated oven for about 10–12 minutes. Remove the foil and the baking weights and return the pastry shell to the oven for a further 5–8 minutes to dry out completely. Reduce the oven temperature to 325°F.

Reserve ¼ cup of the Parmesan. Layer the sliced potatoes and butter in the baked tart shell, seasoning each layer with some of the remaining Parmesan, chives, nutmeg, salt, and pepper.

Put the egg and cream into a bowl, beat well, then pour the mixture over the potatoes. Sprinkle the reserved Parmesan over the top. Bake in the still-hot oven for about 1 hour (it may take up to 15 minutes longer, depending on the type of potato used) or until the potatoes are tender and the top is dark golden brown.

Let cool for 10 minutes before serving with smoked salmon or fried bacon, if liked

Note You could speed up the cooking time by precooking the filling in the microwave. Mix the sliced potatoes, pieces of butter, 1 cup of the Parmesan, nutmeg, half the cream, salt, and pepper in a nonmetal bowl. Cover, leaving a small hole for steam to escape, and microwave for 10 minutes on HIGH. Mix in the remaining cream and egg. Carefully spoon the mixture into the pastry case, sprinkling with chives as you go. Finish with the remaining Parmesan cheese and bake for about 30 minutes, until tender.

red curry of roasted fall vegetables

The vegetables here are very earthy and distinctive, sweet and nutty and the parsnip has that delicious slightly bitter edge. Thai basil is more intensely anise flavored than other varieties. It may be hard to find so try a few leaves of fresh tarragon if you have difficulty sourcing it. Do shop around and experiment to find a Thai curry paste that you really like.

4 small new potatoes, halved

1 large carrot, cut into bite-size pieces

1 tablespoon light olive oil

14 oz. pumpkin or butternut squash, peeled, seeded and cubed

1 parsnip, peeled and cut into batons

1 red onion, cut into 8 wedges

1¾ cups coconut milk

2 tablespoons Thai red curry paste

2 tablespoons brown sugar

2 tablespoons Thai fish sauce

1 cup chicken or vegetable stock

a handful of basil leaves (preferably Thai basil)

jasmine rice, to serve (see page 45)

Serves 4

Preheat the oven to 425°F. Put a baking sheet in the oven for 10 minutes to heat.

Put the potatoes and carrot on the hot baking sheet in a single layer, drizzle with the oil, and roast in the preheated oven for 10 minutes. Add the pumpkin, parsnip, and onion to the baking sheet and roast for a further 20 minutes.

Meanwhile, put 1 cup of the coconut milk in a heavy-based saucepan and set over high heat. Bring to a boil then add the curry paste and stir well. Let boil for 4–5 minutes, until the oil starts to separate from the milk. Add the sugar and fish sauce and cook for 2 minutes, until the mixture is very dark.

Add the remaining coconut milk and stock to the pan. Return to a boil then stir in the roasted vegetables and basil. Cook over low heat for 5 minutes to heat the vegetables through, then serve with bowls of fluffy jasmine rice.

harissa-spiced chickpeas with halloumi and spinach

Halloumi is a firm Greek cheese that is delicious eaten when hot and melting. It has a long shelf-life before it is opened, which means you can keep a package tucked away in the fridge and rustle up this delicious dinner dish at short notice. Harissa is a fiery chile paste used in North African cooking.

1 tablespoon olive oil

1 white onion, finely chopped

1 garlic clove, crushed

1 tablespoon harissa paste (see note right)

14-oz. can chickpeas, drained

14-oz. can chopped tomatoes

5 oz. halloumi cheese, cut into cubes

a large handful of baby spinach leaves

sea salt and freshly ground black pepper

freshly squeezed juice of ½ a lemon

freshly grated Parmesan cheese, to serve

warmed Indian naan bread, to serve

Serves 2

Pour the oil into a large saucepan and set over low heat. Add the onion and garlic and gently sauté until softened. Add the harissa paste, chickpeas, and chopped tomatoes and stir to combine. Bring to a boil then reduce the heat and let simmer for about 5 minutes.

Add the halloumi cheese and spinach, cover, and cook over a low heat for a further 5 minutes. Season to taste and stir in the lemon juice. Spoon onto serving plates and sprinkle with the Parmesan cheese. Serve immediately with warmed naan bread for mopping up the sauce.

Note: If you don't have harissa paste, you can make your own by mixing together ½ teaspoon cayenne pepper, 1 tablespoon ground cumin, 1 tablespoon tomato paste, and the freshly squeezed juice of 1 lime.

winter vegetable gratin

8 oz. celeriac, peeled and cut into cubes

1 carrot, peeled and cut into rounds

1 parsnip, peeled and cut into semi-circles

1 small rutabaga, peeled and cut into chunks

2 potatoes, cut into chunks

1 cup light cream

1 garlic clove, crushed

1 teaspoon mustard powder

½ cup fresh rye or whole-wheat bread crumbs

2 tablespoons finely grated Parmesan cheese

2 teaspoons marjoram leaves

2 tablespoons butter, melted

sea salt and freshly ground black pepper

a shallow ovenproof dish, buttered

Serves 6

This is a great way to use up any combination of root vegetables, especially those that are often overlooked like rutabaga and parsnip.

Preheat the oven to 350°F.

Bring a large saucepan of lightly salted water to a boil. Add the celeriac, carrot, parsnip, rutabaga, and potatoes. Cook for 10 minutes, drain well and transfer to a large bowl.

Put the cream, garlic, and mustard powder in a small saucepan and set over medium heat. Cook, stirring constantly, for about 10 minutes until the mixture is thick and coats the back of a spoon. Season to taste and pour over the vegetables. Spoon the vegetables into the prepared baking dish.

Put the bread crumbs, Parmesan, and marjoram in a bowl and mix to combine. Sprinkle the bread crumb mixture over the vegetables and drizzle the melted butter over the top.

Cook in the preheated oven for about 40 minutes, until the bread crumbs are golden and the mixture around the edge of the baking dish has formed a golden crust. Serve warm, not hot, as a vegetarian main or as a side dish with any roast meat.

tomato and eggplant gratin with tomato and chili pesto

2 eggplants

1 lb. ripe tomatoes

about ⅔ cup olive oil

¼ cup freshly chopped basil

1¼ cups freshly grated Parmesan cheese

sea salt and freshly ground black pepper

tomato and chili pesto

1 large red bell pepper

1½ cups basil leaves

1 garlic clove, crushed

2 tablespoons pine nuts, toasted

2 very ripe tomatoes

6 sun-dried tomatoes in oil, drained

3 tablespoons tomato paste

1 teaspoon mild chili powder

½ cup grated Parmesan or pecorino cheese

⅔ cup extra virgin olive oil

a shallow ovenproof dish, buttered

Serves 4

A deliciously spicy and satisfying vegetarian dish. Any leftover tomato and chili pesto can be spooned into a jar, covered with a thin layer of olive oil, and kept in the refrigerator for up to 2 weeks. It's great with pasta or grilled meat and fish.

Using a sharp knife, cut the eggplant into ¼-inch slices. Sprinkle with salt and put in a colander to drain for 30 minutes. Rinse well and pat dry with paper towels.

Preheat the oven to 425°F.

To make the tomato and chili pesto, put the red bell pepper on a baking sheet and cook in the preheated oven for about 15 minutes, turning often until the skin is starting to blacken and puff up. Transfer it to a clean plastic bag and let cool. When the pepper is cool enough to handle peel off most of the blackened skin, pull out the stalk, and scrape out the seeds. Put the flesh in a food processor with the basil, garlic, pine nuts, tomatoes, sun-dried tomatoes, tomato paste, chili powder, and Parmesan and blend until smooth. With the machine running, slowly pour in the olive oil until well blended. Set aside until needed.

Preheat the oven to 400°F.

Heat the broiler. Brush the eggplant with olive oil and grill on both sides until brown. Drain on paper towels. Cut the tomatoes in half through the middle. Arrange a layer of eggplant in the baking dish, followed by a few spoonfuls of pesto, then a layer of tomatoes and the basil. Sprinkle with Parmesan. Season well, then repeat, finishing with a layer of eggplant. Sprinkle over the remaining Parmesan.

Bake in the preheated oven for 25–30 minutes until browned and bubbling on top. Cool slightly, then serve warm with plenty of bread and salad greens, if liked.

taleggio and potato tortilla
with red bell pepper tapenade

The creamy Taleggio cheese packs a super-rich taste punch and makes this tortilla more than enough for four to enjoy as a light meal. The red bell pepper tapenade is a very versatile recipe to have in your repertoire. It can be tossed through cooked pasta, spooned over grilled vegetables, and stirred into soup.

1 tablespoon olive oil

10–12 small, waxy new potatoes, thickly sliced

1 small red onion, roughly chopped

1 cup vegetable stock

1 handful of flatleaf parsley, chopped

4 oz. Taleggio cheese, chopped

2 eggs, lightly beaten

red pepper tapenade

1 large red bell pepper

1 garlic clove, chopped

⅓ cup pine nuts, lightly toasted

2 tablespoons olive oil

½ cup finely grated Parmesan cheese

Serves 4

To make the tapenade, preheat the oven to 425°F. Put a baking sheet in the oven for a few minutes to heat.

Put the red bell pepper on the baking sheet and cook in the preheated oven for about 15 minutes, turning often until the skin is starting to blacken and puff up. Transfer to a clean plastic bag and let cool. When cool enough to handle, peel off the skin, chop the flesh, and put it in a food processor. Add the garlic, pine nuts, and oil and process until smooth. Spoon into a bowl, add the Parmesan and stir to combine.

Put the oil, potatoes, and onion in a skillet with a heatproof handle. Set over high heat and cook for 1 minute. Add the stock and cook for about 10 minutes, until the stock has evaporated. Stir in the parsley and

sprinkle the pieces evenly over the potatoes. Pour the eggs into the pan and cook for about 2–3 minutes, until the tortilla starts to puff up around the edges.

Preheat the broiler to high. Put the skillet under the hot broiler and cook the tortilla for 1–2 minutes, until the top is golden but still wobbly in the center. Spread some of the tapenade over a serving plate and carefully slide the tortilla onto the plate. Cut into slices and serve warm with extra tapenade on the side for spooning.

mountain eggs

This simple yet satisfying dish is popular in the Swiss Alps, where they cook and serve it in small, individual skillets. Ham is traditional, but it is also very good with slices of chorizo sausage.

4 teaspoons olive oil

4 large cooked potatoes, thickly sliced

8 oz. smoked ham, chopped

4 eggs

4 slices Emmental cheese or 1 cup grated Emmental

sea salt and freshly ground black pepper

chopped flatleaf parsley, to serve (optional)

Serves 4

Heat 1 teaspoon of oil in each of 4 small skillets. Add the potatoes and cook for 2 minutes on each side. Stir in the ham.

Crack an egg into each pan. Top with the sliced or grated cheese, sprinkle with salt and pepper, and cook for 2–3 minutes until the egg is just set and the cheese is melting.

Serve immediately, sprinkled with chopped parsley, if using.

spicy potato omelet

4–6 medium potatoes, unpeeled and halved

6–8 eggs

1 teaspoon ground turmeric

1 teaspoon ground cumin

1 teaspoon paprika

½ teaspoon ground coriander

1 handful of flatleaf parsley, finely chopped

1 tablespoon olive oil

sea salt and freshly ground black pepper

Serve 4–6

This Spanish tortilla-style potato omelet can be cut into thin wedges and served as a light meal or as a side dish with grilled food. The entire omelet can be cooked on the stovetop and browned under the broiler, or it can be baked in the oven.

Put the potatoes in a large saucepan with plenty of salted water and bring to a boil. Cook until tender. Drain and refresh under cold running water. When cool enough to handle, peel off the skins and transfer to a bowl and mash well. Beat the eggs into

the potatoes and add the spices and parsley. Season to taste.

Heat the oil in a skillet with a heatproof handle. Tip in the potato mixture making sure it spreads evenly in the pan. Cover and cook over low heat for 10–15 minutes, until the omelet has puffed up and is quite firm around the edges.

Preheat the broiler to high. Place the skillet under the broiler for 3–4 minutes to brown the top of the omelet. Cut into wedges and serve warm.

one-pot wonders

Portuguese lamb stew with piri piri

A huge, colorful stew is very inviting, and this one makes a nice change from the standard repertoire. The marinade is authentic, as is the spicing; the fiery chile heat comes from Portuguese piri piri sauce. Be sure to buy imported Portuguese sauce, not the inferior chain-restaurant brand more widely available; it makes a huge difference to the taste. This dose has been approved by both a panel of chile-lovers and the chile-wary, so it's fine. But piri piri is very hot and heat varies from one brand to another, so beware if you've never tried it. You can always add more after cooking if it's not hot enough. Serve with Plain, Buttery Couscous (see page 77) or boiled rice.

2 lbs. boneless lamb, cubed

2 tablespoons olive oil

1½ tablespoons all-purpose flour

1 lb. waxy potatoes, peeled and cut into large chunks

1 lb. carrots, cut into large pieces

1–2 teaspoons piri piri sauce, to taste

1½ lbs. zucchini, cut into thick rounds

1 red bell pepper, seeded and chopped

14-oz. can chickpeas, drained

sea salt and freshly ground black pepper

marinade

1 white onion, chopped

6 tablespoons sherry vinegar

1½ teaspoons Spanish smoked paprika (pimentón)

4 garlic cloves, sliced

1 large handful of chopped cilantro

1 large handful of chopped flatleaf parsley

1 tablespoon coarse sea salt

a large, flameproof casserole dish

Serves 6

To make the marinade, combine all of the ingredients in a large nonmetal dish. Mix well. Add the lamb and turn to coat thoroughly. Cover with plastic wrap and refrigerate for at least 3 hours or overnight.

Preheat the oven to 375°F.

Heat the oil in a large flameproof casserole dish. When very hot, add the lamb and all of the marinade. Sprinkle with the flour and stir to coat well. Cook the lamb for 3–5 minutes to sear, then stir in 1 cup water. Add the potatoes, carrots, some salt, and piri piri and mix well. Cover with a lid and cook in the preheated oven for 50 minutes.

Add the zucchini and bell pepper and cook for a further 40 minutes. Remove from the oven and stir in the chickpeas. Season to taste, adding more piri piri if necessary. Serve hot with couscous or rice, as liked.

Languedoc beef stew with red wine, herbs, and olives

This is an adaptation of the classic French beef daube. Adding a little extra wine right at the end lifts the winey flavor after the long, slow cooking.

2 lbs. thickly sliced beef chuck or stewing steak

2 tablespoons all-purpose flour

5–6 tablespoons olive oil

1 large white onion, thinly sliced

2 large garlic cloves, crushed

1 tablespoon tomato paste

1¼ cups full-bodied fruity red wine

½ cup beef stock

1 teaspoon herbes de Provence

1 thin strip of orange peel

2 fresh or dry bay leaves

⅔ cup black olives, pitted

3 heaping tablespoons roughly chopped flat leaf parsley

sea salt and freshly ground black pepper

slow-roasted carrots

1 lb. carrots

a pinch of cayenne pepper

2 tablespoons olive oil

a large flameproof casserole dish

a large, shallow ovenproof dish

Serves 4–6

Trim any excess fat from the beef, then cut the meat into large cubes. Put the flour in a shallow dish and season with salt and pepper. Dip the cubes of beef in the flour to coat.

Heat 2 tablespoons oil in a skillet, add the beef and fry on all sides until it is browned. Do this in batches, adding extra oil as you go. Transfer the beef to a large flameproof casserole dish. Heat the remaining oil in the skillet, add the onion and cook for 3–4 minutes until softened but not browned. Add the garlic and tomato paste and cook

for 1 minute, stirring. Add 1 cup of the wine, the stock, herbes de Provence, orange peel, and bay leaves. Bring to a boil, then pour the sauce into the casserole dish with the beef. Heat the casserole over medium heat and bring the sauce back to a boil. Reduce the heat, cover, and simmer very gently for 2½–3 hours until the meat is completely tender. Check the contents of the casserole dish occasionally to ensure there is enough liquid (add a little extra stock or water if it's dry.)

About two-thirds of the way through the cooking time, prepare the slow-roasted carrots. Preheat the oven to 350°F. Cut the carrots into long, thick diagonal slices. Put the carrots, salt, and cayenne pepper in a large, shallow ovenproof dish, pour the oil over and toss well. Bake in the preheated oven for 45–60 minutes until the carrots are soft and their edges caramelized.

About 30 minutes before the stew is ready, stir in the olives. Just before serving, season to taste then stir in the parsley and the remaining wine and cook for a further 5 minutes. Serve with the slow-roasted carrots on the side.

smoky hotpot of great northern beans

This is a hearty hotpot packed with fall vegetables and rich with smoky paprika. Great northern beans are large and white, resembling butter beans in shape but with a distinctive, delicate flavor. If you can't find them, large butter beans will do just as well.

½ cup dried great northern beans or large butter beans

2 tablespoons olive oil

1 large white onion, chopped

2 garlic cloves, chopped

2 teaspoons Spanish smoked paprika (pimentón)

1 celery rib, chopped

1 carrot, chopped

2 medium waxy potatoes, cut into dice

1 red bell pepper, seeded and chopped

2 cups vegetable stock

sea salt and freshly ground black pepper

crusty bread, to serve

Serves 4

Soak the dried beans in cold water for at least 6 hours or overnight. Drain and put in a large saucepan with sufficient just-boiled water to cover. Cook for 30 minutes until softened. Drain and set aside until needed.

Put the oil in a large saucepan and set over medium heat. Add the onion and cook for 4–5 minutes until softened. Add the garlic and paprika to the pan and stir-fry for 2 minutes. Add the celery, carrot, potatoes, and bell pepper and cook for 2 minutes, stirring constantly to coat the vegetables in the flavored oil. Add the stock and beans and bring to a boil. Reduce the heat and partially cover the pan with a lid. Let simmer for 40 minutes, stirring often, until all the vegetables are cooked. Season to taste and serve with plenty of crusty bread.

vegetable ragù
with spiced couscous

This is a substantial dish packed with nutritious root vegetables. The method for making the spiced couscous is not the traditional Moroccan way, but it does produce a full-flavored version that makes the perfect accompaniment to this ragù.

3 tablespoons olive oil

2 tablespoons butter

1 red onion, chopped

1 celery rib, roughly chopped

6 garlic cloves, lightly smashed

2 cups passata (sieved tomatoes)

2 cups vegetable stock

2 tablespoons oregano leaves

1 parsnip, peeled and chopped

2 carrots, peeled and chopped

6 small, waxy, new potatoes

spiced couscous

1½ cups vegetable stock

2 tablespoons butter

2 cups couscous

1 teaspoon each of ground cumin, ground coriander, and Spanish smoked paprika (pimentón)

¼ teaspoon cayenne pepper

Serves 4

Put the oil and butter in a large saucepan and set over high heat. When the butter sizzles, add the onion, celery, and garlic. Reduce the heat, partially cover the pan and cook for 10 minutes, stirring often, until the vegetables are soft and lightly browned. Add the passata, stock, and oregano and bring to a boil. Reduce the heat to a simmer and cook, uncovered, for about 20 minutes. Add the parsnip, carrots, and potatoes to the pan and cook for a further 15–20 minutes until the vegetables are tender.

To make the spiced couscous, put the stock and butter in a medium saucepan and set over high heat. Bring to a boil, then reduce the heat to low and keep the stock warm. Put the couscous and spices in a large heavy-based saucepan and cook over medium/high heat until the spices are aromatic and just start to turn a dusky brown. Turn off the heat. Pour the warm stock into the pan. Stir, cover with a tight-fitting lid, and let sit for 10 minutes. Fluff up the couscous with a fork, cover again, and let sit for a further 5 minutes. Tip the couscous out into a bowl and fluff up to separate as many grains as possible.

To serve, spoon the couscous onto serving plates and top with the vegetable ragù.

boeuf bourguignon

Although Boeuf Bourguignon sounds as if it should be made from red Burgundy, you'll get a better result if you use a fuller-bodied red wine from the Rhône or Languedoc. Ideally, it should be made a day ahead to allow the flavors to fully develop, but it's not essential to do so.

2 lbs. beef chuck or stewing steak

3 tablespoons olive oil

5 oz. cubed pancetta

3 white onions, finely chopped

2 large garlic cloves, finely chopped

1½ tablespoons all-purpose flour

2 cups full-bodied red wine, plus an extra splash if needed

a bouquet garni made from a few sprigs of thyme, parsley stalks, and a fresh or dried bay leaf

2 tablespoons butter

9 oz. brown or cremini mushrooms, cleaned and halved

2 tablespoons finely chopped flatleaf parsley

salt and freshly ground black pepper

a large, flameproof casserole dish

Serves 6

Pat the beef dry, trim off any excess fat or sinew, and cut into large cubes. Put 1 tablespoon of the oil in a large skillet and set over medium heat. Add the pancetta and fry until lightly browned. Remove from the pan with a slotted spoon and transfer to a large, flameproof casserole dish. Add the beef to the skillet in 2 batches and brown it in the fat that remains in the pan. Transfer to the casserole with the pancetta. Add the remaining oil to the pan and fry the onion gently, covered, until soft and caramelized (about 25 minutes), adding the garlic halfway through the cooking time. Stir the flour into the onions, cook for 1 minute, then add the wine and bring to a boil. Pour over the meat in the casserole dish, add the bouquet garni, and return to a boil. Turn down the heat and simmer over very low heat for 2–2½ hours, until the meat is just tender. Turn off the heat and leave the casserole overnight.

The next day bring the casserole back to boiling point, then turn down low again. Heat the butter in a skillet and fry the mushrooms until lightly browned (about 5 minutes.) Tip the mushrooms into the dish, stir, and cook for another 10–15 minutes. Season the casserole to taste, adding an extra splash of wine if you don't think the flavor is quite pronounced enough. Sprinkle over chopped parsley before serving with Pomme Purée (see page 104) or boiled new potatoes.

pork in cider
with potatoes and apples

If it has apples and cream in it, then it must be a dish from Normandy in France. The cider is a good clue as well, and it provides a luxuriously rich sauce for the long-simmered pork. This is a great dish for all the family, as children (and adults) enjoy sweet things to accompany their meat. Any leftover cider can be enjoyed with the meal.

6 tablespoons unsalted butter

2 white onions, sliced

1 tablespoon sunflower oil

1 pork middle leg roast or fresh ham (about 3½ lbs.), fat trimmed

1½ quarts hard dry cider

2 sprigs of thyme

1¾ lbs. waxy new potatoes, peeled and halved lengthwise

½ cup heavy cream

coarse sea salt and freshly ground black pepper

5 tart apples, such as Braeburn or Cox's, peeled, cored, and sliced

a large, flameproof casserole dish

Serves 4

Put 2 tablespoons of the butter in a large, flameproof casserole dish and set over low heat. Add the onions and cook gently until softened but not browned, about 5 minutes. Remove with a slotted spoon and set aside. Add the oil and increase the heat. Add the pork and cook until browned all over. Remove and season well.

Preheat the oven to 300°F.

Add some of the cider to the casserole dish, heat, and scrape the bottom of the pan. Return the pork and onions to the casserole and add the remaining cider and the thyme. Season lightly and bring to a boil. Boil for 1 minute, skim off any foam that rises to the surface, then lower the heat and cover with a lid. Transfer to the preheated oven and cook for 4 hours. Turn the pork regularly, tasting and adjusting the seasoning half-way through cooking. About 1 hour before the end of the cooking time, add the potatoes and return to the oven. Remove the casserole from the oven, transfer the pork and potatoes to serving plates and cover with foil to keep warm.

Set the casserole over high heat and cook to reduce the liquid slightly, about 10–15 minutes. Season to taste.

To cook the apples, put the remaining butter in a large skillet and set over high heat. Add the apples and cook until browned and tender, 5–10 minutes. Do not crowd the pan; use 2 pans if necessary. To serve, slice the pork and arrange on plates with the potatoes and apples. Stir the cream into the sauce and serve immediately.

Mexican pork and beans

This is a version of chili that's not too spicy and made with pork instead of beef. Serve it with a big bowl of green rice and some warmed tortillas for a fun family feast.

1 white onion, coarsely chopped

4 garlic cloves, coarsely chopped

1 red bell pepper, seeded and coarsely chopped

1 fresh fat red chile, seeded and chopped

2 teaspoons mild chili powder

1 teaspoon Spanish smoked paprika (pimentón)

1 teaspoon ground cumin

1 teaspoon ground coriander

½ teaspoon ground cinnamon

1 teaspoon dried oregano

1¼ cups lager beer

1 lb. pork or beef steak

4 tablespoons sunflower oil

14-oz. can chopped tomatoes

1½ cups passata (sieved tomatoes)

14-oz. can pinto beans or black-eyed peas, drained and rinsed

1 oz. very dark bittersweet chocolate, chopped

sea salt and freshly ground black pepper

green rice

1½ cups basmati rice

4 tablespoons any coarsely chopped green herbs

1 cup frozen chopped spinach, thawed

1 tablespoon safflower oil

to serve

2 avocados, chopped and tossed with lime juice

4–6 soft flour tortillas, warmed

tomato salsa

sour cream

Serves 4–6

Put the onion, garlic, bell pepper, fresh chile, chili powder, paprika, cumin, coriander, cinnamon, and oregano in a food processor. Add half the lager and blend to a purée.

Trim the pork steaks, then cut into large cubes. Heat the oil in a large saucepan, and working in batches, add the pork and fry until browned. Transfer to a plate.

Add the purée to the pan and cook, stirring continuously, over moderate heat or 5 minutes—making sure it doesn't catch and burn. Add the remaining lager, tomatoes, passata, pork, and any juices. Season well and bring to a boil. Reduce the heat and simmer gently, half-covered,

for 30–35 minutes until the pork is tender and the sauce thickened. Gently stir in the beans and chocolate and heat through.

To make the green rice, bring a very large saucepan of cold salted water to a boil. Rinse the rice under cold running water until the water runs clear. Drain. Add the rice to the boiling water, return to a rolling boil and stir once. Boil for exactly 8 minutes then drain well, return to the pan, stir in the herbs, spinach, and oil, then quickly put on a tight-fitting lid. Let steam in its own heat for another 10 minutes, then lightly fluff up with a fork.

Serve the Mexican pork with the green rice and your choice of trimmings.

chili with all the trimmings

Forget the stuff that's slopped on baked potatoes—this is the real thing, made with chopped chuck steak instead of ground hamburger meat and spiced with several types of chile. This is great party food because it should be served in bowls and eaten with a spoon—easy to do even if you are standing up!

1 chipotle chile (dried smoked jalapeño)

4 tablespoons olive oil

4 bell peppers (1 red, 1 yellow, 1 orange, and 1 green), seeded and chopped

1 large red onion

2 celery ribs, chopped

½–1 fresh green chile, finely chopped

2 lbs. chuck steak, cut into small cubes

3 garlic cloves

1 cup red wine, fresh beef stock, or water

¼ teaspoon dried hot pepper flakes

2 teaspoons ground cumin

2 teaspoons dried oregano

2 x 14-oz. cans chopped tomatoes

3 x 14-oz. cans kidney beans, drained and rinsed

1 fresh or dried bay leaf

coarse sea salt and freshly ground black pepper

to serve

2 avocados, chopped and tossed with lime juice

a bunch of scallions, chopped

a bunch of cilantro, chopped

8–12 soft flour tortillas, warmed

sour cream

freshly grated cheese, such as mild cheddar or Monterey jack

lime wedges

Tabasco sauce

Serves 6–8

Put the chipotle in a small bowl and just cover with hot water. Soak for at least 15 minutes, or as long as it takes to prepare the other ingredients.

Heat 2 tablespoons of the oil in a large saucepan. Add the bell peppers, onion, celery, green chile, and a good pinch of salt and cook until soft, 5–7 minutes, stirring often. Remove from the pan and set aside. Increase the heat, add the remaining oil and the meat. Cook, stirring often until browned, 1–2 minutes. Add the garlic and another pinch of salt and cook, stirring constantly for 1 minute. Add the wine and bring to a boil for 1 minute.

Return the bell pepper mixture to the pan and stir in the dried hot pepper flakes, cumin, and oregano. Add the tomatoes, beans, bay leaf, and a good pinch of salt and stir well. Remove the chipotle from the soaking liquid, chop finely and stir into the pan, along with the soaking liquid. Cover and simmer gently until the meat is tender, 15–20 minutes. Season to taste.

At this point, the chili is ready, but you should set it aside for at least 2–3 hours before serving to let the flavors develop or, ideally, make a day in advance and chill until needed. Serve hot, with the trimmings on the side in separate bowls.

classic lamb tagine with almonds, prunes, and apricots

A tagine is a stew which gets its name from the conical, lidded, earthenware cooking dish traditionally used in Morocco. There's no need to worry if you don't have a tagine, a lidded casserole dish is fine.

1–2 tablespoons olive oil

2 tablespoons blanched almonds

2 red onions, finely chopped

2–3 garlic cloves, finely chopped

a thumb-size piece of fresh ginger, peeled and finely chopped

a pinch of saffron threads

2 cinnamon sticks

1–2 teaspoons coriander seeds, crushed

1 lb. boned lamb, from the shoulder, leg or shanks, trimmed and cubed

12 pitted prunes and 6 dried apricots, soaked in cold water for 1 hour and drained

3–4 strips orange peel

1–2 tablespoons dark, runny honey

1 handful of cilantro leaves, chopped

sea salt and freshly ground black pepper

Plain, Buttery Couscous (see opposite), to serve

a flameproof casserole dish or tagine

Serves 4–6

Heat the oil in the base of a flameproof casserole dish. Add the almonds and cook, stirring, until they turn golden. Add the onions and garlic and fry until they begin to color. Stir in the ginger, saffron, cinnamon sticks, and coriander seeds. Add the lamb to the casserole dish and cook for about 1–2 minutes, stirring to make sure it is coated in the onion and spices.

Pour in enough water to just cover the meat then bring it to a boil. Reduce the heat, put the lid on the casserole and simmer for 1 hour, until the meat is tender. Add the prunes, apricots, and orange peel, replace the lid and simmer for a further 15–20 minutes. Stir in the honey, season to taste, cover, and simmer for a further 10 minutes. Make sure there is enough liquid in the pot as you want the sauce to be syrupy and slightly caramelized, but not dry.

Stir in half of the cilantro and serve immediately, sprinkled with the remaining cilantro and accompanied by a mound of couscous.

lamb tagine with chestnuts, saffron, and pomegranate seeds

2 tablespoons unsalted butter

2 white onions, finely chopped

4 garlic cloves, finely chopped

a thumb-size piece of fresh ginger, peeled and finely chopped

a pinch of saffron threads

1–2 cinnamon sticks

2 lbs. lean lamb, from the shoulder or leg, cut into bite-size pieces

8 oz. peeled chestnuts

1–2 tablespoons dark, runny honey

sea salt and freshly ground black pepper

seeds of 1 pomegranate, pith removed

1 handful of mint leaves, chopped

1 handful of cilantro leaves, chopped

Plain, Buttery Couscous (see below), to serve

a flameproof casserole dish or tagine

Serves 4

This is a lovely winter dish, decorated with ruby-red pomegranate seeds. Whole, meaty chestnuts are often used in Arab-influenced culinary cultures as a substitute for potatoes. You can use freshly roasted nuts or ready-peeled, vacuum-packed or frozen chestnuts.

Heat the butter in a flameproof casserole or tagine. Add the onions, garlic, and ginger and sauté until they begin to color. Add the saffron and cinnamon sticks, and toss in the lamb. Pour in enough water to almost cover the meat and bring it to a boil. Reduce the heat, cover with a lid, and simmer gently for about 1 hour.

Add the chestnuts and stir in the honey. Cover with the lid again and cook gently for a further 30 minutes, until the meat is very tender. Season to taste and then stir in some of the pomegranate seeds, mint, and cilantro. Sprinkle the remaining pomegranate seeds and herbs over the lamb, and serve with a mound of couscous.

plain, buttery couscous

2 cups couscous, rinsed and drained

½ teaspoon fine sea salt

1⅔ cups warm water

2 tablespoons safflower or olive oil

3 tablespoons chilled butter, broken into pieces

2–3 tablespoons blanched, flaked almonds

Serves 4–6

Traditionally, plain, buttery couscous, piled high in a mound, is served as a dish on its own after a tagine or roasted meat. It is held in such high esteem that religious feasts and celebratory meals would be unthinkable with it. The par-boiled couscous available outside Morocco is extremely easy to prepare, making it a practical accompaniment for many dishes.

Preheat the oven to 350°F.

Tip the couscous into an ovenproof dish. Stir the salt into the water and pour it over the couscous. Leave the couscous to absorb the water for about 10 minutes.

Using your fingers, rub the oil into the couscous grains to break up the lumps and aerate them. Scatter 2 tablespoons of the butter over the surface and cover with a piece of foil or wet baking parchment. Put the dish in the preheated oven for about 15 minutes, until the couscous is heated through. Meanwhile, prepare the almonds. Melt the remaining butter in a heavy-based skillet over medium heat, add the almonds and cook, stirring, until they turn golden. Remove from the pan and drain on paper towels. Take the couscous out of the oven and fluff up the grains with a fork. Tip it onto a plate and pile it high in a mound, with the toasted almonds scattered over the top.

spicy carrot and chickpea tagine
with turmeric and coriander

Legumes of all kinds and, in particular, chickpeas, make nourishing and simple to prepare winter meals. To avoid lengthy preparation and cooking, use canned chickpeas.

3–4 tablespoons olive oil

1 white onion, finely chopped

3–4 garlic cloves, finely chopped

2 teaspoons ground turmeric

1–2 teaspoons cumin seeds

1 teaspoon ground cinnamon

½ teaspoon cayenne pepper

½ teaspoon freshly ground black pepper

1 tablespoon dark, runny honey

3–4 medium carrots, sliced on the diagonal

2 x 14-oz. cans chickpeas, rinsed and drained

sea salt and freshly ground black pepper

1–2 tablespoons rosewater (optional)

1 handful of cilantro leaves, finely chopped

plain yogurt, to serve

lemon wedges, to serve

a flameproof casserole dish or tagine

Serves 4

Heat the oil in a flameproof casserole dish or tagine. Add the onion and garlic and gently sauté until soft. Add the turmeric, cumin, cinnamon, cayenne, black pepper, honey, and carrots. Pour in enough water to cover the base of the casserole and cover with a lid. Cook gently for 10–15 minutes.

Add the chickpeas, check that there is still enough liquid at the base of the tagine, adding a little water if necessary. Cover with the lid, and cook gently for a further 5–10 minutes. Season to taste, sprinkle the cilantro over the top, and add a dollop of yogurt. Serve with lemon wedges.

winter vegetable tagine with apple and mint

3 tablespoons olive oil

1 white onion, chopped

2 garlic cloves, chopped

½ teaspoon turmeric

½ teaspoon paprika

1 teaspoon ground cumin

1 cinnamon stick

14-oz. can chopped tomatoes

1 large carrot, peeled and cut into thick batons

1 parsnip, peeled and chopped

1 turnip, peeled and cut into rounds

5 oz. sweet potato, peeled and cut into cubes

1 green apple, peeled, cored, and cut into 8 wedges

1 small handful of mint leaves, roughly chopped

sea salt and freshly ground black pepper

Plain, Buttery Couscous (see page 77), to serve

a flameproof casserole dish or tagine

Serves 4

Put the oil in a flameproof casserole dish and set over medium heat. Cook the onion and garlic, stirring, for 2–3 minutes. Add the turmeric, paprika, cumin, and cinnamon and cook for about 2 minutes, until aromatic but not burning.

Add 3 cups water and the tomatoes and season well. Bring to a boil, add the carrot and parsnip, and cook over medium heat, uncovered, for 30 minutes. Add the turnip, sweet potato, and apple and cook for 20–30 minutes, until all the vegetables are tender, then stir in the mint. Serve hot with a mound of couscous.

Aromatic, sweet, succulent, and juicy with the addition of the fruit, this is a perfect introduction to the aromatic spices and flavors typical of Moroccan food. The rich spices work very well with the full-flavored winter root vegetables used here. They all grow under the ground so have been given a breath of air by the addition of some crisp green apple and fresh mint.

a big pot of cassoulet

This hearty dish from south-west France will become a firm favorite. It is big and filling, and traditionally made with a type of haricot bean (lingots.) However, dried butter beans with their creamy texture work just as well, but remember you'll need to soak them before you start cooking. All the components of the dish can be made a day in advance, then assembled on the day. It reheats very well (top up with a little more liquid if it looks dry) and is a boon for entertaining a crowd without any fuss. Make this for large gatherings on cold winter days.

4 cups dried butter beans

1 lb. smoked Italian pancetta or slab bacon, in a piece

4 tablespoons olive oil

4 boneless duck breasts, halved crosswise, or chicken legs or thighs

1½ lbs. fresh Toulouse sausages or Italian coarse pork sausages, cut into 3 pieces each

2 white onions, chopped

1 large carrot, chopped

4–6 large garlic cloves, crushed

3 fresh or dried bay leaves

2 teaspoons dried thyme

2 whole cloves

3 tablespoons tomato paste

12 sun-dried tomatoes in oil, drained and coarsely chopped

1½ cups fresh white bread crumbs

4 tablespoons butter

sea salt and freshly ground black pepper

salad greens, to serve

a large, deep casserole dish

Serves 6–8

Put the butter beans in a very large bowl, cover with plenty of cold water (to cover them by their depth again) and let them soak for at least 6 hours or ideally overnight.

Drain the beans well and tip into a large saucepan. Cover with fresh water, bring to a boil, then simmer for about 1 hour or until just cooked. Drain well (reserving the cooking liquid.)

Trim and discard the rind from the pancetta, and cut the flesh into large pieces. Heat 2 tablespoons of the oil in a skillet. Add the pancetta and, working in batches, brown and transfer to a plate. Heat the remaining oil in the pan, add the duck breasts and fry them skin-side down until the skin is golden. Transfer to the same plate as the pancetta. Brown the sausages in the same way and add to the plate.

Add the onions to the pan, then the carrot, garlic, bay leaves, thyme, cloves, tomato paste, and sun-dried tomatoes. Cook for 5 minutes until softening.

Preheat the oven to 350°F.

To assemble the dish, put half the beans in a large, deep casserole dish. Add an even layer of all the browned meats, then the onion and tomato mixture. Season well. Cover with the remaining beans, then add enough reserved hot cooking liquid until the beans are almost covered. Sprinkle evenly with bread crumbs and dot with butter.

Bake the cassoulet in the preheated oven for about 1 hour, until a golden crust has formed on the top.

Serve warm straight out of the dish with salad greens on the side, if liked.

smoky sausage and bean casserole

The Italians use a mixture of onions, carrots, and celery sautéed in olive oil as the base for many classic soups and casseroles. This holy trinity of veggies is known as a *soffritto* and it's right at home here in a hearty stew with sausages and beans. This is perfect one-pot comfort food.

1 tablespoon olive oil

12 chippolata sausages

1 garlic clove, chopped

1 leek, thinly sliced

1 carrot, diced

1 celery rib, diced

14-oz. can chopped tomatoes

1 teaspoon Spanish smoked paprika (pimentón)

2 tablespoons maple syrup

2 fresh thyme sprigs

14-oz. can cannellini beans, drained and rinsed

sea salt and freshly ground black pepper

4 slices of toasted sourdough bread, to serve

a large heavy-based saucepan

Serves 4

Heat the oil in a large heavy-based saucepan set over high heat. Add the sausages in two batches and cook them for 4–5 minutes, turning often until cooked and evenly browned all over. Remove from the pan and set aside.

Add the garlic, leek, carrot, and celery and cook for 5 minutes, stirring often. Add the tomatoes, paprika, maple syrup, thyme, beans, and 2 cups water and return the sausages to the pan. Bring to a boil, then reduce the heat to medium and simmer for 40–45 minutes, until the sauce has thickened. Season well.

Put a slice of toasted sourdough bread on each serving plate and spoon the casserole over the top to serve.

Variation: Try replacing the sausages with 1 lb. pork neck fillet cut into 1-inch pieces. Cook the pork in batches for 4–5 minutes each batch, turning often so each piece is evenly browned. Return all the pork to the pan, as you would the sausages, and simmer for 45–50 minutes until the pork is tender.

coq au vin

This classic French recipe is a terrific dish for a dinner party because it tastes even better the day after it's made so you can prepare it ahead. The French would always use a local wine to make it but any good, dry, fruity red would work.

10 oz. shallots

3 tablespoons all-purpose flour

6 large skinless, boneless chicken breasts

3 tablespoons olive oil

5 oz. cubed pancetta or chopped thick-cut bacon

2 garlic cloves, thinly sliced

¼ cup brandy

3 fresh thyme sprigs

1 fresh or dried bay leaf

1 x 750-ml bottle dry, fruity red wine

9 oz. small button mushrooms

1 tablespoon butter, softened (optional)

3 tablespoons chopped flatleaf parsley

sea salt and freshly ground black pepper

Pomme Purée (see page 104), to serve

a large, lidded skillet

Serves 6

Cut the shallots into even-sized pieces, leaving the small ones whole and halving or quartering the others.

Put 2 tablespoons flour in a shallow dish and season it with salt and pepper. Dip the chicken breasts in the flour and coat both sides. Heat 2 tablespoons of the olive oil in a large lidded skillet. Add the chicken and fry for 2–3 minutes on each side until lightly browned (you may need to do this in several batches).

Remove the chicken from the pan, discard the oil and wipe the pan with paper towels. Return the pan to the heat and pour in the remaining oil. Add the pancetta and the shallots and fry until lightly browned. Stir in the garlic, then return the chicken to the pan. Put the brandy in a small saucepan and heat it until almost at a boil. Set it alight with a long kitchen match and carefully pour it over the chicken. Let the flames die down, then add the thyme and bay leaf and pour in enough wine to just cover the chicken. Bring back to simmering point, then reduce the heat, half cover the pan, and simmer very gently for 45 minutes. (If you're making this dish ahead of time, take the pan off the heat after 30 minutes, let cool and refrigerate overnight.) Add the mushrooms to the pan and cook for another 10–15 minutes.

Remove the chicken from the pan, set aside and keep it warm. Using a slotted spoon, scoop the shallots, pancetta cubes, and mushrooms out of the pan and keep them warm. Increase the heat under the pan and let the sauce simmer until it has reduced by half. If the sauce needs thickening, mash 1 tablespoon soft butter with 1 tablespoon flour to give a smooth paste, then add it bit by bit to the sauce, whisking well after each addition, until the sauce is smooth and glossy.

Return the shallots, pancetta, and mushrooms to the pan. Season to taste. To serve, cut each chicken breast into 4 slices and arrange them on warmed serving plates. Spoon a generous amount of sauce over the chicken and sprinkle with chopped parsley. Serve immediately with Pomme Purée on the side, if liked.

pumpkin and Gorgonzola risotto

The secret of making a good Italian risotto is to use quality ingredients—fresh butter, best quality risotto rice, and a good flavorful stock are all essential. Roasted pumpkin retains its deep flavor and unique texture here as it's cooked separately, then added to a basic risotto. Tart yet creamy Gorgonzola cheese makes the perfect pairing with the sweet pumpkin. You could substitute any firm, dense winter squash—such as butternut or hubbard.

1 lb. pumpkin, peeled, seeded, and diced

1 tablespoon olive oil

4 cups vegetable stock

2 tablespoons unsalted butter

1 leek, halved lengthwise and thinly sliced

1 garlic clove, chopped

1½ cups Arborio (risotto) rice

2 oz. Gorgonzola cheese, crumbled

sea salt and freshly ground black pepper

a small roasting pan

Serves 4

Preheat the oven to 350°F.

Put the pumpkin in a small roasting pan, drizzle with the olive oil, season, and toss to coat in the oil. Roast in the preheated oven for about 30 minutes, until soft and golden.

Put the stock in a saucepan and heat until gently simmering. Melt the butter in a saucepan set over high heat and add the leek and garlic. Cook for 4–5 minutes, stirring often, until the leeks have softened.

Add the rice to the pan and stir for 1 minute, until the rice is well coated with oil. Add ½ cup of the hot stock to the rice and cook, stirring constantly, until the rice has absorbed most of the liquid. Repeat this process until all the stock has been used. This will take about 20–25 minutes. The rice should be soft but still have a slight bite to the center. Add the roasted pumpkin to the pan. Remove from the heat, stir in the Gorgonzola, and serve immediately.

roasted butternut squash risotto

Risotto is a relatively simple dish to make but a good deal of stirring is required. Remember to keep the stock hot and the heat constant. Roasting the squash first brings out its sweetness and the pumpkin seeds add a spicy crunch.

1 lb. butternut squash, peeled, seeded, and diced

3 tablespoons olive oil

1½ teaspoons dried hot pepper flakes

2 tablespoons pumpkin seeds

3½ cups vegetable stock

1 small onion, finely chopped

¾ cup Arborio (risotto) rice

½ cup white wine

½ cup finely grated Parmesan cheese

crème fraîche or sour cream, to serve (optional)

sea salt and freshly ground black pepper

a small roasting pan

Serves 2

Preheat the oven to 450°F.

Put the squash in a small roasting pan with 1 tablespoon of the olive oil and ½ teaspoon of the dried hot pepper flakes. Season well and toss to coat in the oil. Roast in the preheated oven for about 20 minutes, until soft and golden.

Heat 1 tablespoon of the remaining olive oil in a small skillet and toast the pumpkin seeds with the remaining dried hot pepper flakes for about 1–2 minutes until lightly browned. Set aside until needed.

Whilst the squash is cooking in the oven, make the risotto. Pour the vegetable stock into a large pan and heat to a simmer. Pour the remaining oil into a saucepan and set over medium heat. Gently sauté the onions for about 1 minute, or until softened but not colored. Add the rice, stir for 2–3 minutes, then add the wine and let simmer until

reduced by half. Add another ladleful of hot stock. Let the risotto continue to simmer gently, adding another ladleful of stock each time the liquid has been absorbed into the rice. Stir, continuously, until the rice has absorbed all the stock.

Once the rice is cooked and tender, stir in the roasted squash and the Parmesan and season to taste. Serve immediately, topped with a dollop of crème fraîche, if using, and sprinkled with the spicy toasted pumpkin seeds.

mushrooms, cognac, and cream risotto

Here is a rich, creamy risotto that is very substantial and comforting. The cognac adds a touch of indulgent luxury, making it perfect for a special occasion or entertaining.

1 stick unsalted butter

9 oz. brown or cremini mushrooms, thinly sliced

1 tablespoon Cognac or other brandy

3 tablespoons light cream

4 cups vegetable stock

1 tablespoon olive oil

8 shallots, finely chopped

2 garlic cloves, crushed

1½ cups Arborio (risotto) rice

1½ cups freshly grated Parmesan cheese

a handful of flatleaf parsley, coarsely chopped

sea salt and freshly ground black pepper

shavings of Parmesan cheese, to serve

Serves 4

Heat half the butter in a skillet until foaming, then add the mushrooms and cook for 5 minutes. Season. Add the Cognac, boil until reduced by half, then stir in the cream. Let simmer for about 5 minutes, until the sauce has thickened slightly. Set aside.

Put the stock in a saucepan. Heat until almost boiling, then reduce the heat until barely simmering to keep it hot.

Heat the remaining butter and oil in a large skillet or heavy-based saucepan set over medium heat. Add the shallots and cook for 1–2 minutes, until softened but not browned. Add the garlic.

Add the rice and stir for about 1 minute, until the grains are well coated and glistening.

Add 1 ladleful of hot stock and simmer, stirring continuously, until it has been absorbed. Continue to add the stock at intervals and cook as before, until the liquid has been absorbed and the rice is tender but firm to the bite. This should take about 18–20 minutes.

Add the mushroom mixture, grated Parmesan, and parsley. Season to taste. Remove from the heat and let rest for 2 minutes before serving. Spoon into bowls, top with Parmesan shavings and serve.

country chicken

A simple-to-make yet delicious roast chicken dish that is served with pasta.

1 chicken, about 4 lbs., cut into 8 pieces

8 shallots

5 fresh or dried bay leaves

9 oz. thick-cut bacon, chopped

2 tablespoons olive oil

1½ tablespoons whole-grain mustard

1 bunch of tarragon, coarsely chopped

½ cup white wine

sea salt and freshly ground black pepper

cooked tagliatelle, to serve

Serves 4

Preheat the oven to 350°F.

Put the chicken in a bowl and add the shallots, bay leaves, bacon, and oil. Season well, mix and transfer to a roasting pan. Cook in the preheated oven for 30 minutes.

Put the mustard, tarragon, and wine in a small bowl and mix well. Remove the chicken from the oven and pour off any excess fat. Pour the mustard mixture over the chicken and return it to the oven for a further 10 minutes. Serve with the tagliatelle.

roasts

italian-style roast pork
with white wine, garlic, and fennel

A great recipe for weekend entertaining or a family get-together. You can leave the meat gently bubbling away for hours in the oven and you will have a fantastic roast at the end of the day. An Italian wine like Pinot Grigio is best, but you could use any dry white wine.

6½ lbs. boned, rolled shoulder of pork

2 tablespoons fennel seeds

1 tablespoon coarse sea salt

1 teaspoon black peppercorns

1 teaspoon crushed dried chiles

6 garlic cloves, roughly chopped

freshly squeezed juice of 2 lemons

2 tablespoons olive oil

¾ cup dry white wine

to serve

sautéed or mashed potatoes

green beans or salad greens

a large roasting pan with a rack

an ovenproof dish

Serves 8

Preheat the oven to 450°F.

Cut deep slits in the pork skin with a sharp knife. Grind the fennel seeds, salt, peppercorns, and chiles in a mortar using a pestle. Add the chopped garlic and pound to a rough paste. Using your hands, smother the paste all over the pork working it into the slits. Put the pork on a wire rack and place it over a roasting pan. Cook, skin-side up in the preheated oven for 30 minutes. Remove the pork from the oven and reduce the heat to 250°F.

Turn the pork over and pour half the lemon juice and all of the olive oil over it. Return the pork to the oven and cook for at least 7 hours, checking it every couple of hours. You should be aware that the meat is cooking—it should be sizzling quietly. Ovens vary, so you may want to increase the temperature slightly. About halfway through the cooking time, spoon off the excess fat and squeeze the remaining lemon juice over the meat. About 30 minutes before the pork is due to be cooked, remove it from the oven and increase the heat to 425°F. Transfer the pork, skin side up, to a clean ovenproof dish and when the oven is hot, return the pork to the oven for about 15–20 minutes to crisp up the crackling. Remove from the oven and let rest.

Pour off any excess fat from the original roasting pan and add the wine and ⅔ cup water. Heat gently on the stovetop, working off any sticky burnt-on bits from the edges of the pan and simmer for 10 minutes. Strain the juices through a strainer and keep warm.

Carve the pork into thick slices. Put a few slices on warmed plates and pour some of the pan juices over the top. Serve with sautéed potatoes and salad greens or mashed potatoes and green beans, as preferred.

pork loin roasted with rosemary and garlic

This classic Tuscan dish is redolent of the early morning markets where "porchetta" is sold crammed into huge rolls, this dish re-creates all those tastes and smells in your oven at home. Use plenty of rosemary so that the sweet pork flesh will be suffused with its pungent aroma.

3 lbs. boneless, center-cut pork loin (ask the butcher to remove the skin and score it for crackling, but to give you the bones.)

6 garlic cloves

4 tablespoons rosemary needles

1¼ cups dry white wine

a few sprigs of rosemary

olive oil, for brushing

sea salt and freshly ground black pepper

2 roasting pans

kitchen twine

Serves 6

Preheat the oven to 450°F.

Weigh the meat and calculate the total cooking time, allowing 25 minutes for every 1 lb.

Turn the loin fat-side down. Make deep slits all over. Put the garlic, rosemary, and at least a teaspoon of salt and pepper into a food processor and blend to a paste. Push this paste into all the slits in the meat and spread the remainder over the surface of the meat. Roll up and tie securely with kitchen twine.

Put the pork in a hot skillet and brown all over. Set in a roasting pan. Pour the wine over the pork and tuck in the rosemary sprigs.

Put the bones in the other roasting pan, convex side up. Rub the skin with a little oil and salt, then drape it over the bones. Put the tin on the top shelf of the oven, and the pork loin on the bottom or middle shelf. Roast for 20 minutes. Reduce the heat to 400°F, and roast for the remaining calculated time, basting the pork loin every 20 minutes. Rest the pork for 15 minutes before carving. Serve slices of pork with shards of crackling and spoon the pan juices over the top. Serve with roast potatoes, if liked.

roasted pork
with apple and fennel puddings

They may sound a little unusual but these savory puddings packed with vegetables and sweet raisins make a wonderful accompaniment to pork.

3 lbs. pork loin roast in one piece, skin on

2 tablespoons white wine vinegar

1 tablespoon sea salt

apple and fennel puddings

3 tablespoons butter

1 white onion, chopped

1 celery rib, thinly sliced

1 tart green apple, grated

1 fennel bulb, grated

1 cup fresh bread crumbs

⅓ cup raisins

1 egg, lightly beaten

1 cup chicken or vegetable stock

⅓ cup slivered almonds

a large roasting pan with a rack

an ovenproof dish, lightly buttered

Serves 6

Make small incisions on the skin of the pork with a sharp knife, but don't cut through to the meat. Rub the vinegar and sea salt into the skin and set aside for 1 hour at room temperature. (This will help the skin dry out making for better crackling.)

Preheat the oven to 425°F. Put the pork on a cooking rack over a roasting pan. Pour 1 cup water into the tin and cook in the preheated oven for 30 minutes. Reduce the oven temperature to 350°F and cook for a further 1½ hours, until the pork skin is golden and crisp. Keep adding water to the roasting pan during the cooking time

as necessary. Remove the pork from the oven, cover with foil, and let rest for 10 minutes.

To make the puddings. Heat the butter in a skillet set over medium heat. When the butter is sizzling, add the onion and celery and cook for 4–5 minutes, stirring often. Add the apple and fennel and cook for 1 minute, stirring well. Remove the pan

from the heat and add all the remaining ingredients, except for the almonds. Stir well.

Spoon the mixture into the baking dish, sprinkle the almonds on top and cook in a preheated oven at 350°F for 1 hour. Serve slices of the pork with slices of the pudding and Slow-cooked Sprouts with Pancetta and Chestnuts (see page 108), if liked.

roast turkey with lemon and herb stuffing

Family tradition will dictate the best way to present a festive turkey. This recipe has a light herb and lemon bread stuffing made with plenty of butter. It absorbs lots of juices and is fabulous served cold the next day. Allow 40 minutes at the end of cooking for the turkey to rest before carving.

a 10–12-lbs. turkey, with giblets (trussed weight)

1 white onion, coarsely chopped

a sprig of thyme

1 bay leaf

1 stick salted butter

sea salt and freshly ground black pepper

lemon and herb stuffing

2 eggs

1 stick plus 1 tablespoon butter, melted

a handful of parsley leaves

1 teaspoon lemon thyme leaves

grated peel and juice of 1 lemon

4½ cups fresh white bread crumbs

sea salt and freshly ground black pepper

squares of cheesecloth, baking parchment, or foil (enough to cover the breast and drumsticks)

a large roasting pan

Serves 10–12

To make a stock, the day before, put the giblets, minus the liver, but with the neck chopped in half, in a saucepan. Add the onion, thyme, and bay leaf. Cover with water and bring slowly to a boil, removing any foam as it rises. Simmer for 2 hours and strain. Taste and, if necessary, reduce to strengthen the flavor. Set aside.

To make the stuffing, put the eggs, butter, parsley, thyme, grated lemon peel, and juice in a liquidizer and blend to a smooth purée. Pour it over the bread crumbs and mix well. Season to taste and set aside. Wipe out

the neck area and body cavity of the turkey with a damp cloth and season the inside. Spoon in the stuffing, allowing plenty of room for it to expand. This is especially true when stuffing the neck.

Put half the butter in a saucepan and melt gently. Using your hands, spread the remaining butter all over the skin. Soak the cheesecloth or paper in the melted butter and drape over the bird, with a double layer covering the drumsticks.

Preheat the oven to 425°F. Put the turkey in a roasting pan in the middle of the oven and roast for 35 minutes. Reduce the oven temperature to 335°F and roast for about 3½ hours. Return to the oven temperature to 425°F. Remove the coverings from the

bird and cook for 30 minutes to crisp and brown the skin. Remove the turkey from the oven, cover with a tent of foil, and leave to rest in a warm place for 40 minutes.

Remove the foil and using oven gloves, tip out any free juices from the cavity, then lift the turkey onto the serving platter. Return it to the oven, leaving the door open until the temperature has dropped and will no longer cook the bird. Pour off the gravy juices, preferably into a gravy separator or pitcher to lift off the fat. Reheat with the seasoned stock. Use to fill a gravy boat, reserving the rest in a Thermos for second servings.

Serve with the traditional trimmings of your choice, such as candied yams, green beans, cranberry relish, roast potatoes, and corn bread.

pot roast brisket with red wine

¾ cup full-bodied red wine, such as Zinfandel

¾ cup fresh beef stock or made with ½ a beef stock cube, cooled

2 tablespoons red wine vinegar

1 large garlic clove, crushed

1 fresh or dried bay leaf

1 white onion, chopped

a few of sprigs of thyme or ½ teaspoon dried thyme

3½ lbs. boned, rolled brisket of beef

2–3 tablespoons safflower oil or light olive oil

2 tablespoons dry Marsala or Madeira

sea salt and freshly ground pepper

a large flameproof casserole dish

Serves 6

Brisket has a rich flavor that lends itself well to braising. You can use any full-bodied red wine, but Zinfandel has just the right gutsy rustic character.

Put the wine, stock, wine vinegar, garlic, bay leaf, onion, and thyme in a large pitcher and mix. Put the meat in a plastic bag, pour in the marinade. Knot the top of the bag or seal with a wire tie. Leave the meat to marinate in the fridge for at least 4 hours or preferably overnight.

Preheat the oven to 400°F.

Remove the meat from the marinade and dry thoroughly with paper towels. Strain the marinade and reserve the liquid. Heat the oil in a flameproof casserole dish. Brown the meat all over in the hot oil then add 3–4 tablespoons of the strained marinade. Put a lid on the casserole dish and roast in the preheated oven for 2 hours. Check from time to time that the pan juices are not burning. Add more marinade if necessary, but the flavor of this dish comes from the well-browned sticky juices, so do not add too much extra liquid. If on the other hand more liquid has formed, spoon some out. Simmer the remaining marinade over low heat until it loses its raw, winey taste.

Once the meat is cooked, let rest in a warm place. Spoon any fat off the surface of the pan juices and add the Marsala and the cooked marinade. Bring to a boil, scraping the tasty brown bits from the side of the casserole and adding water if necessary. Season to taste. Serve slices of the meat with the sauce poured over the top.

roast beef rib-eye with winter vegetables and garlic crème

Unlike roast pork, where the fat and skin form tasty crackling, excess fat on beef can be off-putting. Choose a lean fillet and cook it quickly for a lovely rare roast.

1¾ lbs. beef rib-eye boneless roast

1 tablespoon freshly ground black pepper

1 bunch of baby carrots, unpeeled and tops trimmed

2 small red onions, cut into thin wedges

1 turnip, cut into quarters

½ small celeriac, cut into thick batons

1 large parsnip, cut into semi circles

1 tablespoon light olive oil

garlic crème

1 bulb of garlic

3 egg yolks

1 teaspoon Dijon mustard

1 teaspoon red wine vinegar

1 cup light olive oil

Serves 4

Preheat the oven to 350°F.

To make the garlic crème, wrap the garlic firmly in foil and cook in the preheated oven for 40 minutes. Remove and let cool. Cut in half and squeeze the soft flesh directly into the bowl of a food processor. Add the egg yolks, mustard, and vinegar and process until smooth. With the motor running, add the olive oil in a steady stream until all the oil is incorporated. Transfer to a small bowl, cover, and chill until needed.

Rub the pepper all over the beef. Cover and refrigerate, for at least 3 hours or overnight.

When ready to cook the beef, preheat the oven to 425°F and put a baking sheet in the oven to heat. Put the vegetables on the baking sheet, drizzle with olive oil, and roast in the preheated oven for 30 minutes, turning once. Cover with foil to keep warm.

Set a skillet over high heat. When smoking hot, add the beef and sear for 4 minutes, turning every minute. Put it in a roasting pan and roast in the still-hot oven for 10 minutes. Turn the beef and cook for a further 5 minutes. Cover with foil and let rest for 10 minutes before carving. Serve with the roast vegetables and garlic crème.

roast beef tenderloin
with soy and butter sauce

The soy and butter sauce may sound unconventional, but it makes a very light, savory, meaty sauce that is much more wine friendly than some of the very intense winey reductions you get in restaurants.

1 teaspoon coarse sea salt

2 teaspoons black peppercorns

½ teaspoon ground allspice

1 tablespoon all-purpose flour

1½ lbs. beef tenderloin in a piece

1 tablespoon safflower oil or light olive oil

3 tablespoons softened butter

2 tablespoons Madeira or dry Marsala

1½ cups fresh beef stock or stock made with ¾ beef stock cube

1½ tablespoons Japanese soy sauce, such as Kikkoman

a large cast-iron casserole dish or deep roasting pan

Serves 6

Preheat the oven to 425°F.

Put the salt and peppercorns in a mortar and grind with a pestle until finely ground. Mix in the allspice and flour. Remove any fat or sinew from the beef and dry thoroughly with paper towels. Put the seasoning and flour on a plate and roll the beef in the mixture, patting it evenly into the surface and shaking off any excess. Set the casserole dish over medium/high heat, add the oil and half the butter, and brown the beef quickly on all sides. Transfer to the preheated oven and roast for 20–40 minutes, depending how thick

your piece of beef is and how rare you like it. Remove from the oven and set aside for 10–15 minutes, lightly covered with foil. Pour off any excess fat in the pan, leaving about 1 tablespoon. Pour in the Madeira and let it bubble up for a few seconds, then add the stock and soy sauce. Bring to a boil, turn the heat down a little, and reduce by half. Pour any juices that have accumulated under the meat into the pan, whisk in the remaining butter and season with pepper (you shouldn't need any salt).

Carve the meat into slices and serve with the sauce and some roast new potatoes and green beans, if liked.

perfect roast beef with
herbed Yorkshire puddings

The tenderloin is the most tender cut of beef. Resting the meat before carving will ensure a juicy result. The Yorkshire puddings are a traditional English side and worth trying.

2 lbs. beef tenderloin in a piece

olive oil

8 oz. thinly sliced pancetta or sliced dry-cure bacon

sea salt and freshly ground black pepper

herbed Yorkshire puddings

1⅔ cups all-purpose white flour

½ teaspoon salt

2 large rosemary sprigs, chopped

1 tablespoon chopped fresh thyme

4 eggs

2¾ cups milk

8 tablespoons beef dripping, duck fat or safflower oil

kitchen twine

a 12-cup muffin pan or Yorkshire pudding pan

Serves 6

To make the Yorkshire puddings, sift the flour and salt into a food processor or blender. Add the rosemary and thyme, eggs, and milk. Blend until smooth and pour into a pitcher. Cover and refrigerate for at least 1 hour.

Trim the beef of all fat and membrane and neatly tie at regular intervals to give a good shape. Rub all over with olive oil, salt, and pepper. Wrap with the pancetta. Cover and set aside for 20 minutes at room temperature.

Preheat the oven to 450°F.

Put the meat in a roasting pan and cook in the preheated oven for 25 minutes for medium rare; 20 for very rare; 35 for medium. Remove from the oven, cover loosely with foil, and let rest in a warm place for 10–15 minutes (this will make it easier to carve and give the meat an even pink color.)

Lower the oven temperature to 400°F and cook the puddings while the meat is resting. Put the dripping into the holes of the muffin pan and heat in the oven for a couple of minutes. Stir the batter and pour into the hot pan—it should sizzle as soon as it hits the fat. Return to the oven and bake for 15–20 minutes until well-risen and deep golden brown—do not open the oven during cooking if you want a perfect result!

Carve the meat into thick slices and serve with the Yorkshire puddings and the juices from the meat.

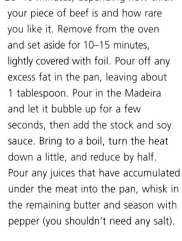

pot roast leg of lamb
with rosemary and onion sauce

This is the perfect cook-and-forget roast. The lamb is cooked until tender on a bed of rosemary and onions. The meat juices are then puréed with the soft onions to make a rich sauce.

3 lbs. leg of lamb

2 tablespoons olive oil

3 garlic cloves, crushed

2 tablespoons chopped rosemary needles

3 large rosemary sprigs

2 fresh bay leaves

4 large white onions, thinly sliced

1¼ cups dry white wine

2 teaspoons Dijon mustard

sea salt and freshly ground black pepper

Creamy Potato Gratin (see page 104), to serve (optional)

a large flameproof casserole dish

Serves 6

Trim the lamb of any excess fat. Heat the oil in a casserole dish in which the lamb will fit snugly. Add the lamb and brown it all over. Remove to a plate and let cool.

Crush the garlic and chopped rosemary needles together in a mortar with a pestle. Using a sharp knife, make small incisions all over the lamb. Push the paste deep into these incisions. Season well.

Preheat the oven to 325°F.

Put the rosemary sprigs, bay leaves, and onions in the casserole and put the lamb dish on top. Mix the wine with the mustard, then pour into the casserole. Bring to a boil, cover tightly, then cook in the preheated oven for 1½ hours, turning the lamb twice.

Increase the oven temperature to 400°F and remove the lid from the casserole dish. Cook for a further 30 minutes.

The lamb should be tender and cooked through. Transfer the lamb to a serving plate and keep warm.

Skim the fat from the cooking juices and remove the bay leaves and rosemary sprigs. Add a little water if too thick, then bring to a boil, scraping the bottom of the pan to mix in the sediment. Pour the liquid into a blender and whizz until smooth. Season to taste. Serve the lamb with the sauce and Creamy Potato Gratin, if liked.

roasted rack of lamb with a spicy crust

3 tablespoons cumin seeds

2 tablespoons coriander seeds

2 teaspoons black peppercorns

4 cloves

4 small dried red chiles

2 tablespoons sea salt

finely grated peel and freshly squeezed juice of 2 lemons

¼ cup olive oil

3 racks of lamb, 6 chops each

¾ cup red wine

Petits Pois à la Française (see page 106) and Perfect Mashed Potatoes (see page 103), to serve (optional)

a large roasting pan

Serves 8

Racks of lamb are so convenient as they cook much more quickly than a large leg of lamb. Do trim as much fat off as possible as it doesn't get a chance to crisp up under the spicy crust. Allow two to three chops per person, depending on the size.

Heat a skillet and add the cumin and coriander seeds, peppercorns, cloves, and chiles. Cook for 1 minute, stirring. Tip into a mortar and crush coarsely with a pestle. Transfer to a small bowl and stir in the salt, grated lemon peel and juice, and oil.

Put the racks of lamb into a large roasting pan. Rub the spice mixture well into the lamb. Cover and chill overnight.

Preheat the oven to 400°F.

Cook the lamb in the preheated oven for 20 minutes then reduce the oven temperature to 350°F. Cook for a further 20 minutes for rare lamb; 25 minutes for medium; 35 minutes for well done. Remove the lamb from the oven, transfer to a carving board and let rest for 5 minutes in a warm place.

Meanwhile, add the wine and ¾ cup water to the roasting pan and set over high heat. Stir to scrape up all the roasted bits on the bottom, and boil until reduced by half.

To serve, cut the lamb into chops, spoon the sauce over the top, and serve with Petis Pois and Perfect Mashed potatoes, if liked.

baked and glazed ham

Ham is an easy dish to prepare for a large gathering and children love it. Buy a ready-boned ham to make carving simple. A 2-lb ham will allow you leftovers to serve cold in salads and sandwiches during the following week.

2 lbs. cured ham, soaked overnight

2 tablespoons English or Dijon mustard

2 tablespoons brown sugar

1 teaspoon crushed cloves

freshly ground black pepper

a large roasting pan, lightly oiled

Serves 4

Preheat the oven to 325°F.

Put the ham in a large roasting pan and cover with a sheet of foil. Cook in the preheated oven for 1 hour.

Remove from the oven and discard the foil. Drain off the cooking juices and peel off the skin, leaving a layer of fat. Using a knife, score the fat with a criss-cross pattern.

Spread the mustard evenly over the ham. Mix the sugar, cloves, and pepper in a small bowl, then sprinkle the mixture all over the ham, pressing it down into the fat with your hands.

Return the ham to the oven and bake for 20 minutes. Serve hot, warm, or cold.

roast chicken with bay leaves, thyme, and lemon

This poor man's version of a dish in which truffle slices are stuffed under the chicken skin makes a nice change from ordinary roast chicken. The bay leaves and thyme delicately flavor the flesh, while the tart lemon keeps it lively.

a 3-lb chicken

2 lemons, 1 quartered, 1 sliced

6 large fresh bay leaves

2 thyme sprigs

1–2 tablespoons extra virgin olive oil or 2 tablespoons unsalted butter

1 teaspoon dried thyme

1 white onion, sliced into rounds

1 cup dry white wine

1 tablespoon unsalted butter

coarse sea salt and freshly ground black pepper

Vichy Carrots (see page 106) and Crunchy Roast Potatoes (see page 102), to serve (optional)

a large roasting pan with a rack

Serves 4

Season the inside of the chicken and stuff with the lemon quarters, 2 of the bay leaves, and the thyme. Using your fingers, separate the skin from the breast meat to create a pocket and put 1 bay leaf on each side of the breast, underneath the skin. Put the remaining bay leaves under the skin of the thighs. Rub the outside of the chicken with oil or butter, season generously, and sprinkle all over with the dried thyme.

Preheat the oven to 425°F.

Put the chicken on its side on a rack set over a roasting pan. Add water to the pan to a depth of ½ inch and add the sliced lemon and onion. Cook in the preheated oven for 40 minutes, then turn the chicken on its other side. Continue roasting the chicken until cooked through and the juices run clear when a thigh is pierced with a skewer, about 40 minutes more. Add extra water to the pan if necessary during cooking. Remove from the oven, remove the chicken from the rack to a plate and let rest, covered in foil, for 10 minutes. Add

1 cup water, or the wine if using, to the pan juices and cook over high heat, scraping the bottom of the pan, for 3–5 minutes. Stir in the butter. Carve the chicken, spoon over the pan juices and serve with Vichy Carrots and Crunchy Roast Potatoes, if liked.

roasted pheasant breasts
with bacon, shallots, and mushrooms

Pheasant is by far the most plentiful and popular of game birds. While cooking a whole pheasant is more economical, it does involve all that last-minute carving and it never looks as good when plated as a breast does. If you are offered a choice between hen and cock pheasant, buy the hen—the meat will be more tender. As pheasant season is October through to January, this makes an extra special seasonal treat.

6 boneless and skinless pheasant breasts

12 slices of smoked, rindless bacon

6 thyme sprigs

3 fresh bay leaves, halved

2 tablespoons unsalted butter

1 tablespoon olive oil

12 shallots

½ cup dry sherry

6 portobello mushrooms, quartered

6 thick slices French bread

8 oz. watercress

sea salt and cracked black pepper

a large roasting pan

Serves 6

Preheat the oven to 375°F.

Wrap 2 slices of bacon around each breast, inserting a thyme sprig and half a bay leaf between the pheasant and the bacon.

Put the butter and oil in a large roasting pan and set over high heat. Add the breasts, shallots, sherry, mushrooms, and season. Turn the breasts in the mixture until they are well coated. Transfer the pan to the preheated oven and roast for 25 minutes. Remove from the oven and let rest for 5 minutes. Put the bread onto serving plates, then add a little watercress, the mushrooms, shallots, and pheasant. Spoon over any cooking juices and serve immediately.

roast monkfish with pancetta, rosemary, and red wine gravy

Monkfish makes an excellent alternative to a meaty roast, especially when it is served with a robust red wine gravy. It also makes an impressive entrée for a dinner party.

8 rosemary sprigs

7 garlic cloves

4 tablespoons butter at room temperature, plus an extra 2 tablespoons, chilled and cubed

2 small monkfish tails (about 1 lb. each), skinned, boned, and each divided into 2 fillets

4 oz. very thinly sliced pancetta or dry-cure bacon, rind removed

2 tablespoons olive oil

8 shallots, quartered

¾ cup full-bodied fruity red wine, such as Merlot

½ cup chicken or vegetable stock

sea salt and freshly ground black pepper

Smashed Roast New Potatoes (see page 102) and salad greens, to serve

a roasting pan

Serves 4–6

Strip the needles from 4 of the rosemary sprigs, chop them finely, and transfer to a bowl. Crush 1 garlic clove and add it to the rosemary along with the softened butter. Season and beat well.

Preheat the oven to 400°F.

Lay out the monkfish fillets in pairs with the thin end of 1 fillet next to the thick end of the other. Spread the rosemary and garlic butter over one side of each fillet, then press each pair together with the buttered sides in the middle. Wrap the slices of pancetta around each pair of fillets, enclosing them completely. Put 1 tablespoon olive oil in a roasting pan, then add the monkfish. Put the remaining garlic cloves, rosemary, and shallots around the monkfish, then drizzle over the remaining oil. Roast in the preheated oven for 25 minutes, turning the shallots and garlic halfway through, until the pancetta or bacon is nicely browned.

Remove the monkfish from the pan, lightly cover with foil, and set aside. Leaving the shallots and garlic in the pan, pour off all but 1 tablespoon of the oil and butter, then set the pan over medium heat. Heat for a few minutes, stirring, then pour in the wine. Let it bubble up and reduce by half, then add the stock. Continue to let it bubble until the liquid is reduced by half again. Strain the gravy through a strainer and return it to the pan. Reheat gently, then whisk in the chilled butter. Season to taste

Cut the monkfish into thick slices, arrange on serving plates, and spoon over the red wine gravy. Serve with Smashed Roast New Potatoes and salad greens, if liked.

roasted salmon wrapped in prosciutto

What makes this dish such a joy is that you will have no last-minute dramas with the fish falling to pieces, because the prosciutto not only adds flavor and crispness, it also parcels up the salmon and makes it easier to handle.

4 thin slices Fontina cheese, rind removed

4 skinless salmon fillets (about 8 oz. each)

4 fresh or dried bay leaves

8 thin slices prosciutto

sea salt and freshly ground black pepper

Garlic Sautéed Green Beans (see page 115), to serve (optional)

Serves 4

Preheat the oven to 400°F. Trim the Fontina slices to fit on top of the salmon fillets. Put a bay leaf on top of each fillet, then a slice of the Fontina. Wrap 2 slices of prosciutto around each piece of salmon, so that it is covered. Transfer to a baking sheet.

Cook in the preheated oven for about 10–15 minutes, until the fish is cooked through and the prosciutto crispy. Serve with Garlic Sautéed Green Beans, if liked.

sides and salads

smashed roast new potatoes

This is great way to roast baby new potatoes. You will need tiny little ones to make these perfect roasties. The initial blast of a really hot oven is what makes the potatoes so soft and fluffy on the inside and about to burst out of their crispy skins.

16 small new potatoes, unpeeled

2 tablespoons light olive oil

a few rosemary sprigs

sea salt flakes, to sprinkle

a non-stick roasting pan

Serves 4

Preheat the oven to 450°F. Put the roasting pan in the oven to heat up for 10 minutes.

Put the potatoes in a large bowl with about 1 tablespoon of the oil and toss to coat. Put the potatoes in the hot roasting pan and roast in the preheated oven for 20 minutes.

Remove the pan from the oven and turn the potatoes over. Gently press down on each potato with the back of large metal spoon until you hear the potato skin pop.

Drizzle the remaining oil over the potatoes, add the rosemary sprigs, and sprinkle with the salt. Return to the oven for a further 10 minutes, until the potatoes are crispy and golden brown.

Variation: Remove the potatoes from the oven and spoon over a soft French cheese (such as a sweet and nutty brie), while the potatoes are still warm. The cheese will melt and transform these into an indulgence treat. Delicious served with a Baked and Glazed Ham (see page 97.)

crunchy roast potatoes

Use an old, floury potato here, such as Maris Piper or King Edward. The idea is to get a crisp, crunchy outside and a light and fluffy inside.

3½ lbs. floury roasting potatoes, peeled and halved or quartered

5–6 tablespoons vegetable oil

sea salt flakes, to sprinkle

a non-stick roasting pan

Serves 6

Preheat the oven to 400°F.

Place the potatoes in a large saucepan. Cover with cold water and bring to a boil. Add a little salt, boil for 5 minutes, then drain. Pour the oil into a roasting pan and tip in the potatoes, turning them in the oil.

Roast the potatoes in the preheated oven for 45 minutes, turning them halfway through the cooking time. Turn the heat up to 425°F and continue to roast until the potatoes are crisp (about another 15–20 minutes.)

perfect mashed potatoes

The secret of perfect mashed potatoes is the right potato—a floury variety that fluffs up properly. Older potatoes work better than new and make sure that they are thoroughly cooked or the mash will be lumpy. Mash will keep warm in a very cool oven (250°F) for up to 2 hours if covered with buttered foil. Otherwise, cool and reheat gently, beating in melted butter and hot milk. If adding herbs, add just before serving.

1½ lbs. floury potatoes, peeled and quartered

4 tablespoons unsalted butter

⅓–½ cup milk

3 tablespoons chopped scallions, sautéed in butter (optional)

2 tablespoons creamed horseradish (optional)

sea salt and freshly ground black pepper

Serves 4

Preheat the oven to 300°F.

Put the potatoes in a saucepan of salted cold water and bring to a boil. As soon as the water comes to a boil, reduce to a simmer (it's important not to cook the potatoes too quickly) and cook for about 20 minutes. When perfectly done, the point of a sharp knife should glide into the center.

Drain in a colander, then set over the hot pan to steam and dry out. Tip the potatoes back into the hot pan and crush with a potato masher or pass them through a mouli or ricer into the pan. Melt the butter in the milk. Using a wooden spoon, beat the butter and milk into the mash—an electric hand-mixer sometimes helps here. Add the scallions and horseradish, if using. Season well, pile into a warm dish, and serve immediately.

buttermilk mash

This simple variation on classic mashed potatoes has creamy buttermilk and Parmesan added to give extra flavor.

1½ lbs. floury potatoes, peeled and quartered

½ cup buttermilk

3 tablespoons unsalted butter

¼ cup finely grated Parmesan cheese

Serves 4

Put the potatoes in a large saucepan of salted cold water and bring to a boil. Cook for about 20 minutes, until tender. Drain and return to the warm pan with the buttermilk and butter. Mash well then beat with a wooden spoon until really smooth. Stir in the Parmesan and season well with sea salt and black pepper.

pomme purée

This decadent French way of cooking potatoes makes a chic alternative to classic mashed potatoes.

2 lbs. red-skinned potatoes, such as Desirée, peeled and cut into quarters or eighths

3 tablespoons heavy cream

¼–⅓ cup full-fat milk

2½ tablespoons unsalted butter, cut into cubes and at room temperature

sea salt and freshly ground black pepper

a potato ricer or mouli

Serves 6

Put the potatoes in a saucepan, pour over boiling water, add 1 teaspoon salt, and bring back to a boil. Turn down the heat and simmer gently for about 12–15 minutes until you can easily pierce them with a skewer. Drain them in a colander, then return them to the pan over very low heat and leave them for 1–2 minutes to dry off.

Mix the cream and milk together and heat until just below boiling point in a separate saucepan. Tip the potatoes back into the colander, then pass them through a potato ricer back into the pan. Pour in half the cream mixture and beat with a wooden spoon, then gradually beat in the remaining cream mixture and the butter. Season well with salt and pepper.

creamy potato gratin

Cream and potatoes are almost all you'll find in this classic French dish. If the recipe included cheese, it wouldn't be a true dauphinois. Serve as a partner for simple roast meat or poultry.

4½ lbs. waxy boiling potatoes, halved if large

2 quarts full-fat milk

1 fresh bay leaf

2 tablespoons unsalted butter

2 cups whipping cream

a pinch of freshly grated nutmeg

coarse sea salt, to sprinkle

an ovenproof baking dish

Serves 4–6

Preheat the oven to 350°F.

Put the potatoes in a large saucepan with the milk and bay leaf. Bring to a boil, then lower the heat, add a pinch of salt, and simmer gently for about 5–10 minutes.

Drain the potatoes. When cool enough to handle (but still hot), slice into rounds about ⅛ inch thick.

Spread the butter in the bottom of the baking dish. Arrange half the potato slices in the dish and sprinkle with salt. Put the remaining potato on top and sprinkle with more salt. Pour in the cream and sprinkle with the grated nutmeg.

Bake in the preheated oven until golden and the cream is almost absorbed, but not completely, 45 minutes. Serve hot.

harissa potatoes

These spicy potatoes made with harissa, a Moroccan chile paste, make an interesting alternative to more classic potato side dishes. Serve them with any roast meat or poultry or grilled fish.

3 tablespoons olive oil

1 onion, sliced

1½ lbs. waxy boiling potatoes, thickly sliced

5 garlic cloves, sliced

1 heaping teaspoon harissa, or more to taste

1 teaspoon ground cumin

1 teaspoon coarse sea salt

1 tablespoon freshly squeezed lemon juice

a large handful of cilantro leaves, chopped

sea salt and freshly ground black pepper

Serves 4

Heat the oil in a large skillet with a lid. Add the onion and cook for 1 minute, then add the potatoes and cook for 2–3 minutes more, stirring often. Add the garlic, harissa, cumin, and salt and mix well. Add enough water to cover by half, then cover with a lid and simmer gently for 20 minutes. Uncover and continue simmering until cooked through and the liquid has been almost completely absorbed, 5–8 minutes more.

Stir in the lemon juice and cilantro, season to taste and serve.

French fries

Choose evenly sized potatoes so that the fries you end up with are roughly the same width and length. Use an electric deep-fryer or a deep saucepan for frying, and add the uncooked fries to the oil in small batches. If using a saucepan, use a sugar thermometer to check the temperature of the oil.

2 lbs. floury roasting potatoes, such as Desirée or King Edwards

sea salt

safflower or peanut oil, for deep-frying

an electric deep-fryer (optional)

Serves 4

Cut the potatoes into ½ inch slices, then cut these slices into ½ inch thick sticks. Put them in a bowl of cold water and let soak for 15 minutes. Drain well and dry thoroughly using a clean, dry kitchen towel.

Pour 2 inches depth of oil into a deep, heavy saucepan. Heat gently until the oil reaches 300°F on a sugar thermometer.

Alternatively, use an electric deep-fryer and follow the manufacturer's instructions. Cook the fries, in batches, for 5–6 minutes until lightly golden and cooked through. Drain on paper towels and set aside until required.

Increase the heat of the oil to 350°F and cook the fries again, in batches, for 1–2 minutes until crisp and golden. Drain on paper towels, transfer to a large bowl, and season lightly with salt. Serve hot.

Variation Shoestring Potatoes
Cut the potatoes into ⅙ inch slices, then again into ⅙ inch thick strips. Rinse well under cold running water and dry thoroughly using a clean, dry kitchen towel. Heat 2 inches depth of oil in a deep, heavy

skillet until it reaches 350°F on a sugar thermometer. Add the potato strips and fry, in batches, for 2–3 minutes until crisp and golden. Drain on paper towels. Serve hot, sprinkled with salt.

carrots with cream and herbs

Thyme is omnipresent in French cuisine. Here, it transforms what would otherwise be ordinary boiled carrots into something subtly sumptuous. The crème fraîche helps too. You can substitute steamed baby leeks for the carrots, but stir in a tablespoon or so of butter when adding the crème fraîche.

2 lbs. carrots, ideally baby ones

3 tablespoons unsalted butter

a sprig of thyme

2 tablespoons crème fraîche or sour cream

several sprigs of chervil

a small bunch of chives

fine sea salt

Serves 4

If using larger carrots, cut them diagonally into 2-inch slices. Put in a large saucepan (the carrots should fit in almost a single layer for even cooking.) Add the butter and set over low heat. Cook to melt and coat, about 3 minutes. Half fill the saucepan with water, then add a pinch of salt and the thyme. Cover and cook until the water is almost completely evaporated, about 10–20 minutes.

Stir in the cream and add salt to taste. Using kitchen scissors, snip the chervil and chives over the top, mix well, and serve.

Variation In early spring, when turnips are sweet, they make a nice addition to this dish. Peel and quarter large turnips, or just peel baby ones—the main thing is to ensure that all the vegetable pieces (carrot and turnip) are about the same size so that they cook evenly. Halve the carrot quantity and complete with turnips. Sprinkle with a large handful of just-cooked shelled peas before serving for extra crunch and a pretty color.

vichy carrots with fresh ginger

These buttery carrots almost caramelize as they cook, so the ginger adds a spicy punch to cut through the rich sweetness.

2 lbs. carrots

2 tablespoons finely chopped fresh ginger

4 tablespoons unsalted butter

½ teaspoon sea salt

2 teaspoons sugar

freshly ground black pepper

3 tablespoons chopped cilantro or parsley

Serves 8

Cut the carrots into batons or rounds and put in a saucepan with the ginger, butter, salt, and sugar. Half-cover with water, bring to a boil and boil steadily, stirring once or twice, until the water has almost disappeared and the carrots are tender.

Reduce the heat and let the carrots brown a little and caramelize. Season with black pepper and stir in the cilantro or parsley. Serve immediately.

petits pois à la Française

Equally good when made with fresh or frozen peas, this recipe is great for large numbers. The lettuce adds sweetness to the peas. Perfect with fish or lamb.

2½ cups green peas, fresh or frozen

1 large white onion, thinly sliced

1 small lettuce, such as Little Gem, shredded

4 tablespoons unsalted butter

1 teaspoon sugar

2 tablespoons chopped mint

2 tablespoons chopped parsley

sea salt and freshly ground black pepper

Serves 4

Mix the peas, onion, and lettuce together in a casserole dish or heavy-based saucepan. Add ⅔ cup water, the butter, sugar, salt, and pepper. Cover tightly with a lid and simmer for 30 minutes, until the peas are tender. Stir in the mint and parsley, season to taste, then serve.

mushrooms marinated with raisins and apple cider vinegar

Mushroom fans will love this tasty mix of juicy mushrooms in a sweet and sour chile-spiked marinade. Add a crumbling of salty cheese, such as feta, and you have a pretty special vegetarian entrée.

¼ cup olive oil

2 shallots, peeled and finely chopped

2 garlic cloves, peeled and crushed

1 lb. cremini mushrooms, halved

1½ tablespoons apple cider vinegar

2 tablespoons raisins

2 tablespoons runny honey

a pinch of dried hot pepper flakes

oregano leaves, to garnish (optional)

Serves 4–6

Heat 3 tablespoons of the olive oil in a skillet. Add the shallots and garlic and gently sauté over low heat for 2–3 minutes, until softened. Add the mushrooms and cook for 4–5 minutes, until golden. Add the vinegar and raisins, and let bubble for 1–2 minutes. Stir in the honey, remaining olive oil, and dried hot pepper flakes. Cook for a further minute. Remove from the heat and let cool. Leave to marinate for 30 minutes before serving. Garnish with oregano, if using.

slow-cooked Brussels sprouts
with pancetta and chestnuts

You won't be surprised to learn that Brussels sprouts are a member of the cabbage family as they look just like little baby cabbages. But unlike cabbage they have a sweet and nutty flavor, especially when they are young. Use baby sprouts in this rather festive dish, which is lovely as a side with roast turkey, pork, or beef. If you can't find pancetta, use chopped thick-cut bacon slices instead.

7 oz. fresh chestnuts

¼ cup light olive oil

2 oz. pancetta, chopped into ½-inch pieces

1 small onion, finely chopped

2 garlic cloves, thinly sliced

¼ cup chicken or vegetable stock

¼ cup dry white wine

1 tablespoon freshly squeezed lemon juice

14 oz. young Brussels sprouts, trimmed

Serves 2

Preheat the oven to 400°F.

Cut a small slit, without cutting into the flesh, along one side of the chestnuts. Put them on a baking sheet and roast in the preheated oven for 15–20 minutes, until the skins start to split. Remove from the oven and let cool a little. Peel and rub off the skin and set aside.

Heat the oil in a heavy-based saucepan over medium heat. Add the pancetta, onion, and garlic and cook for 3–4 minutes. Pour in the stock, wine, and lemon juice and bring to a boil. Add the sprouts to the pan, cover, reduce the heat, and simmer gently for 20 minutes. Turn the sprouts over and add the chestnuts to the pan. Cover and cook for a further 20 minutes, until almost all the liquid has evaporated and the sprouts are tender. Serve immediately.

savoy cabbage with bacon and cream

Based loosely on a traditional French dish that includes pheasant, this recipe is a very elegant way to dress up a rustic vegetable. It seems to go best with poultry and potatoes, both roasted. In fact, it's an idea to make extra cabbage and potatoes because they can be mashed together the next day, formed into patties, and fried in a mix of butter and olive oil for a leftover feast.

1 bay leaf

1 Savoy cabbage, about 3 lbs.

2 tablespoons unsalted butter

1 tablespoon extra virgin olive oil

4 oz. thinly sliced pancetta, chopped

a sprig of sage, leaves stripped and thinly sliced

¼ cup crème fraîche or sour cream

sea salt and freshly ground black pepper

Serves 4

Bring a large saucepan of water to a boil with the bay leaf and a large pinch of salt. Quarter the cabbage and blanch it in the boiling water for 2–3 minutes. Drain well. Core the cabbage quarters, then slice crosswise. Set aside until needed.

Heat the butter and oil in a large skillet. Add the pancetta and sage and cook over high heat, stirring often, for 1 minute. Add the blanched cabbage and a pinch of salt and cook, stirring often, for 2–3 minutes.

Stir in the cream and cook until warmed through, about 1 minute. Mix to thoroughly combine, season to taste, and serve hot.

cauliflower with garlic and anchovies

If you thought cauliflower was boring think again. The Italians have a way with vegetables and know how to cook them beautifully. This deliciously savory recipe breathes new life into what is so often a tired old vegetable side. Perfect with roast meats and poultry. The Tabasco is optional but does add a nice spicy kick.

2 cauliflowers, about 1¼ lbs.

1 bay leaf

3 celery ribs, plus a handful of leaves

3–5 tablespoons extra virgin olive oil

6 anchovy fillets in oil, drained and coarsely chopped

3–4 garlic cloves, finely chopped

freshly squeezed juice of ½ a lemon

sea salt and freshly ground black pepper

Tabasco sauce (optional)

Serves 4

Separate the cauliflowers into florets. Bring a large saucepan of water to a boil with the bay leaf. Add a generous amount of salt, then the cauliflower. Cook for 2–3 minutes just to blanch. Drain and set aside.

Chop the celery ribs finely and set aside, then chop the leaves finely too and set aside. Heat 3 tablespoons of the oil in a large skillet. Add the celery ribs and cook for 1 minute. Add the cauliflower and a good pinch of salt. Cook for 2–3 minutes over medium-high heat, without stirring. The cauliflower should brown.

Add the remaining oil if it seems to need it (this dish can be slightly oily), then the anchovies, and cook for 2–3 minutes more. Add the garlic, stir well, and cook for just 30 seconds—do not let the garlic burn. Remove from the heat and stir in the celery leaves. Add the lemon juice and season to taste. Add a few drops of Tabasco, if using. Serve hot or at room temperature.

spiced cauliflower with red bell pepper and peas

This is a spicy treat that's perfect if you like things hot. The vegetable dishes you find in Indian cuisine are among the most delicious in the world. Many of the recipes embrace the philosophy of cooking fresh produce and letting the flavors speak for themselves.

½ a head of cauliflower, cut into large florets

2 teaspoons ground cumin

1 teaspoon turmeric

3 tablespoons light olive oil

2 teaspoons black mustard seeds

6–8 curry leaves

1 onion, sliced

1 red bell pepper, cored, seeded, and sliced

1 tablespoon finely grated fresh ginger

2 garlic cloves, chopped

1 large green chile, sliced

½ cup vegetable stock

2 ripe tomatoes, chopped

1 cup freshly shelled peas

cooked basmati rice, to serve (optional)

Serves 4

Put the cauliflower florets in a large bowl with the cumin and turmeric and toss until evenly coated in the spices.

Put the oil in a skillet set over medium/high heat. Add the cauliflower, mustard seeds, and curry leaves and cook for 8–10 minutes, turning the pieces often so that they soften and color with the spices.

Add the onion and bell pepper and cook for 5 minutes. Add the ginger, garlic, and chile and stir-fry for 1 minute, then add the stock, tomatoes, and peas. Reduce the heat and let simmer gently for 10 minutes until the vegetables are tender and cooked through.

Spoon over basmati rice to serve, if liked.

sweet potatoes with thyme and chile

Sweet potatoes make such a nice change from the usual vegetable repertoire and their partnership here with chiles and thyme is inspired. Serve them to accompany roast meat or poultry—they are especially good with pan-fried duck breasts.

3 large sweet potatoes, about 1 lb.

2 tablespoons unsalted butter

2 tablespoons extra virgin olive oil

a small bunch of thyme

1 fresh red chile, seeded (optional) and finely chopped

coarse sea salt

a large roasting pan

Serves 4

Preheat the oven to 425°F.

Cut the potatoes into large chunks. Put them in a large roasting pan and toss with the butter and oil. Strip the thyme leaves from the stems and sprinkle them over the potatoes with the chile. Season well with salt and add ½ cup water. Bake in the preheated oven until just browned and tender, about 35–40 minutes. Serve hot.

Note This is not very spicy. To make it hotter, keep the chile seeds in or add an extra chile.

cauliflower gratin

The secret of delicious cauliflower is to blanch it first; if you parboil it with a bay leaf, the unpleasant cabbage aroma disappears. This classic recipe goes especially well with pork or can be enjoyed on it's own as a light meal.

1 large cauliflower, separated into large florets

1 fresh bay leaf

2 cups heavy cream

1 egg, beaten

2 teaspoons Dijon mustard

1½ cups finely grated Comté* cheese

coarse sea salt

a baking dish, greased with butter

Serves 4–6

Preheat the oven to 400°F.

Bring a large saucepan of water to a boil, add the bay leaf, salt generously, then add the cauliflower. Cook until still slightly firm, about 10 minutes. Drain and set aside.

Put the cream in a saucepan and bring to a boil. Boil for 10 minutes. Add a spoonful of hot milk to the beaten egg to warm it, then stir in the egg, mustard, and 1 teaspoon salt.

Divide the cauliflower into smaller florets, then stir into the cream sauce. Transfer to the prepared dish and sprinkle the cheese over the top in an even layer. Bake in the preheated oven for about 40–45 minutes, until golden. Serve hot.

*Note Like Gruyère, Comté is a French mountain cheese but the similarity stops there. Use Emmental or Cantal if Comté is unavailable.

roast beets

Banish all thoughts of vinegary pickled beets from your mind—when slow-roasted in the oven beets are mellow and delicious and make the perfect accompaniment to many dishes.

Preheat the oven to 400°F.

Peel the beets and trim the stems to about 1 inch. Cut into 4–6 wedges, depending on size. Put the wedges in a roasting pan that will hold them in a single layer. Add the vinegar, oil, parsley, oregano, mint, and a good pinch of salt. Toss well.

Cover the dish with foil and roast in the preheated oven for 30 minutes. Remove the foil and continue roasting until just tender when pierced with a knife, about 20 minutes more. There should still be some liquid in the dish; if this evaporates too quickly, add a spoonful or so of water during cooking. Serve hot or at room temperature if preferred.

6 beets, about 1 lb. 10 oz.

3 tablespoons balsamic vinegar

2 tablespoons extra virgin olive oil

a small handful of flatleaf parsley, chopped

a small handful of oregano or dill, chopped

a sprig of mint, leaves chopped

coarse sea salt

a large roasting pan

Serves 2–4

wilted greens

Here are two foolproof ways with greens. Larger greens are good with sausages and roast beef, smaller leaves make an excellent side with roast fish.

2 lbs. greens, mixed or single, such as kale, chard, spinach, mustard greens, or arugula

extra virgin olive oil

1 lemon

1 garlic clove (Method two)

fine sea salt and freshly ground black pepper

Serves 2–4

Method one: Best for larger, robust greens, such as chard. Bring a large saucepan of water to a boil. Salt well, add the greens and blanch for 2–3 minutes. Drain and refresh under cold running water. Let dry in a colander, tossing occasionally to let all the water escape (squeeze excess with your hands if necessary.) To serve, sprinkle with 2–3 tablespoons oil, the juice of ½ a lemon, and a good sprinkling of salt and pepper.

Method two: Best for smaller leaves, such as baby spinach and arugula. Crush the garlic clove, but leave whole and spear on the end of a fork. Heat 2 tablespoons oil in a large skillet. Add a very large handful of leaves and cook, stirring with the garlic fork, until wilted. Using tongs, transfer the leaves to a large plate and continue adding handfuls until all the greens are wilted. Season with extra oil, a squeeze of lemon juice, and plenty of salt and pepper.

butternut squash with pistou

Butternut squash and pistou aren't obvious partners, but the sweetness of squash goes very well with the garlicky basil sauce. This is best served with roast lamb or chicken because the pistou makes a lovely sauce for it all (though you might want to double the quantity to be sure.) Experiment with different types of winter squash, such as kabochka (the small Japanese pumpkins with striped green skin and brilliant orange flesh), or other kinds of pumpkin, in place of the butternut.

6 tablespoons extra virgin olive oil

4 garlic cloves

a large handful of fresh basil leaves

2 butternut squash, about 2 lbs. each

fine sea salt

a large roasting pan

Serves 4

Preheat the oven to 400°F.

To make the pistou, put the oil, garlic, basil leaves, and a pinch of salt in a small food processor. Blend well. Transfer to a small bowl.

Trim the stems from the butternut squash and cut in half lengthwise. Scoop out the seeds. Arrange the squash halves in a roasting pan and sprinkle with salt. Brush generously with the pistou, letting it well up a bit in the cavity if you like. Roast in the preheated oven until just browned at the edges and tender when pierced with a knife, 40–45 minutes. Serve hot, with the remaining pistou.

baked spinach mornay

This is really rich and ideally served with simply cooked meat or fish. It is also a great brunch dish, perfect with poached eggs and hot buttered toast.

3 tablespoons butter

2 tablespoons all-purpose flour

3 cups full-fat milk

7 oz. Fontina cheese, cubed

1 onion, chopped

1 garlic clove, chopped

2 lbs. fresh spinach leaves, chopped

¼ teaspoon freshly grated nutmeg

toasted and buttered sourdough bread, to serve (optional)

Serves 6

Preheat oven to 350°F.

Put 2 tablespoons of the butter in a saucepan and set over medium heat. When sizzling, add the flour and cook for 1 minute, stirring constantly, until a thick paste forms. Reduce the heat to low and slowly pour the milk into the pan, whisking constantly until all the milk is incorporated and the mixture is smooth and lump-free. Add the cheese and stir until it has melted into the sauce.

Heat the remaining butter in a large skillet set over high heat. Add the onion and garlic and cook for 2–3 minutes, until the onion has softened. Add the spinach, cover with a lid, and cook for 4–5 minutes, stirring often, until the spinach has wilted. Transfer the spinach to a large bowl. Pour in the cheese sauce and stir to combine. Spoon the mixture into a large baking dish.

Sprinkle the nutmeg over the top and bake in the preheated oven for 30 minutes until the top is golden and bubbling. Serve hot.

roasted early fall vegetables
with chickpeas

Sometimes we forget how good the simple things can be. These fall vegetables roasted with whole garlic cloves and thyme sprigs make a substantial side or serve them with Plain, Buttery Couscous (see page 77) for a vegetarian entrée.

12 button mushrooms

2 ripe tomatoes, halved

1 red bell pepper, seeded and cut into strips

1 yellow bell pepper, seeded and cut into strips

1 red onion, peeled and cut into wedges

1 small fennel bulb, sliced into thin wedges

1 garlic bulb, broken into individual cloves but left unpeeled

2 teaspoons sea salt

2 tablespoons olive oil

14-oz. can chickpeas, drained and rinsed

2 fresh thyme or rosemary sprigs

Plain, Buttery Couscous (see page 77), to serve (optional)

Serves 4

Preheat the oven to 350°F.

Put the mushrooms, tomatoes, bell peppers, onion, fennel, and garlic in a large roasting pan. Sprinkle the salt evenly over the vegetables and drizzle with the oil. Roast in the preheated oven for 1 hour.

Remove the pan from the oven and turn the vegetables. Add the chickpeas and thyme sprigs. Return the pan to the oven and roast for a further 30 minutes, until the edges of the vegetables are just starting to blacken.

To serve, spoon the Plain, Buttery Couscous, if liked, onto serving plates and top with the warm roasted vegetables with chickpeas.

garlic sautéed green beans

It may seem odd here not to cook the beans in a pan of water, but with this method the beans take on a wonderful buttery, garlic flavor, while keeping their crunchy texture.

2 garlic cloves, crushed and finely chopped

2 tablespoons unsalted butter

2 tablespoons olive oil

8 oz. runner beans, trimmed and cut into 3 pieces each

8 oz. fine green beans, trimmed

8 oz. sugar snap peas, trimmed

freshly ground black pepper

Serves 8

Put the garlic, butter, and oil in a large saucepan and heat gently. When hot, add all the beans and sugar snap peas and cook, stirring frequently, for 5 minutes until tender but still slightly crisp. Sprinkle with plenty of black pepper and serve warm.

beet, goat cheese, and pine nut salad with melba toast

Wintry, festive sumptuousness, thanks to the deep red of the beets and the bright white of the cheese.

12 slices white bread

1½ lbs. small, unpeeled beets, trimmed

1 lb. mixed salad greens

8 oz. firm goat cheese, crumbled

⅓ cup pine nuts, toasted in a dry skillet

a large handful of basil leaves

2 garlic cloves, crushed and chopped

5 tablespoons olive oil

freshly squeezed juice of 2 lemons

salt and freshly ground black pepper

Serves 12

To make the Melba toast, toast the slices of bread, then remove the crusts. Using a large, sharp knife, split each piece of toast through the middle, to give 2 whole slices of toast with 1 soft bread side each. Cut in half diagonally, then cook under a preheated broiler, soft side up, until golden and curled. Watch the toasts carefully, as they can burn quickly.

Preheat the oven to 350°F.

Put the beets in a roasting pan and roast in the preheated oven for 45 minutes. Remove, let cool, then peel and quarter. Put the salad greens onto a serving dish, add the beets and goat cheese, then sprinkle with pine nuts and basil leaves.

Put the garlic, oil, and lemon juice in a small bowl. Season, mix well, and pour over the salad. Serve with the Melba toast.

smoked duck, mandarin, and pecan salad with Pinot Noir dressing

3 mandarin oranges or other small sweet oranges such as clementines

4 oz. mâche or watercress

8 oz. sliced smoked duck breast

⅔ cup candied pecans* or walnuts

Pinot Noir dressing

1 cup Chilean or other inexpensive Pinot Noir, or another fruity red wine

1½ tablespoons light brown sugar

½ cup light olive oil

1 medium pomegranate

½–1 teaspoon pomegranate molasses or balsamic vinegar

sea salt and freshly ground black pepper

Serves 6

Wine can be used instead of vinegar to make a deliciously fruity salad dressing. Making a reduction like this is a thrifty way to use up leftover wine and it will keep in the refrigerator for several days. If you can't find a pomegranate, use sun-dried cherries instead.

Peel and slice the oranges horizontally, reserving any juice. Cut the larger slices in half to make half-moon shapes.

To make the dressing, put the wine in a small saucepan, bring to a boil, then lower the heat. Simmer for 10–15 minutes or until the wine has reduced by two-thirds. Remove the pan from the heat, stir in the sugar, and let cool.

Once cool, whisk in the olive oil and season to taste. Cut the pomegranate in half and scoop the seeds into a bowl, catching any juice. Discard the pith and tip the seeds and juice, along with any juice from the oranges, into the dressing. Add the pomegranate molasses or balsamic vinegar to taste. Stir well.

Divide the mâche or watercress among serving plates and arrange the duck breast and orange slices on top. Scatter over the candied pecans or walnuts. Give the dressing a quick whisk, then spoon it over the salad. Serve immediately.

*Note If you can't find candied pecans, put ⅔ cup pecans in a dry, non-stick skillet and sprinkle over 1 teaspoon sugar. Toast gently over medium heat for a couple of minutes, shaking the pan frequently, until the nuts are crisp and the sugar has caramelized.

chicken, raisin, and chile salad with hazelnut dressing

Everyone will love this moist marinated chicken salad. For the best flavor, be sure to toast the hazelnuts until dark golden. If time is short, you could cheat a little and buy a freshly cooked rotisserie chicken and throw away the evidence!

a 2½-lb. chicken

6 cups chicken or vegetable stock

a handful of raisins

⅔ cup blanched hazelnuts, toasted until dark golden

1 teaspoon dried hot pepper flakes, or to taste

a small bunch of flatleaf parsley, chopped

sea salt and freshly ground black pepper

hazelnut dressing

6 tablespoons hazelnut oil

2 tablespoons red wine vinegar

1 tablespoon sugar

Serves 4–6

Put the chicken in a large saucepan and cover with the stock. Bring to a boil. Turn down the heat and poach the chicken for about 1 hour, or until the juices run clear when the chicken is tested with a skewer at the thickest part of the leg. Leave to cool in the stock, then transfer to a chopping board. Shred the meat into a large bowl. Add the raisins, hazelnuts, and dried hot pepper flakes.

To make the hazelnut dressing, whisk the hazelnut oil, vinegar, and sugar together in a small bowl and season to taste. Add to the chicken along with the parsley, toss well and leave to marinate in a cool place (but not the refrigerator) for at least 1 hour. Serve at room temperature.

winter-spiced salad with
pears, honeyed pecans, and ricotta

You need to be careful when buying ricotta because it can sometimes be very soggy, especially when sold in tubs. Look for the organic varieties or buffalo ricotta which is crumbly rather than creamy. Buffalo mozzarella also works well, as does a soft, fresh goat cheese. Leave some seeds in the chile to give a little kick, awaken all the other flavors, and contrast with the sweet nuts.

1 star anise

1 cinnamon stick

2 pears, unpeeled, quartered and cored

a large handful of salad greens, such as arugula, shredded radicchio, or baby spinach

5 oz. buffalo ricotta

honeyed pecans

¼ cup pecans

¼ teaspoon dried hot pepper flakes

¼ teaspoon fennel seeds

3 tablespoons clear honey

dressing

4 tablespoons safflower oil

1 tablespoon walnut oil

freshly squeezed juice of 1 lemon

1 large red chile, partly seeded and chopped

Serves 4

Fill a saucepan with water and add the star anise and cinnamon stick. Bring to a boil and add the pears. Poach for 12 minutes, or until tender.

Put the pecans, a large pinch of salt, the dried hot pepper flakes, and the fennel seeds in a skillet and toast until golden and aromatic. Pour in the honey, turn the heat right up, and leave to bubble away for a few minutes. Tip onto parchment paper and leave to cool.

Meanwhile, to make the dressing, whisk together the safflower and walnut oils, the lemon juice, and chile.

Transfer the salad greens to serving bowls, arrange the pears on top, and crumble over the ricotta. Drizzle with dressing and roughly break up the nuts and scatter them over the top. Serve immediately.

salad of winter fruit
with blue cheese and spinach

The number of organically grown apple and pear varieties at your local farmers' market might be a little overwhelming! If you are unsure, ask the stallholder what varieties are good for cooking, for munching on or, as here, slicing directly into a salad bowl with a few other great ingredients.

2 apples, cored and cut into thin wedges

2 firm pears, cored and cut into thin wedges

1 small head of radicchio, leaves separated

4 oz. fresh spinach leaves

8 oz. firm blue cheese, crumbled

tarragon vinaigrette

3 tablespoons light olive oil

1 tablespoon tarragon vinegar

¼ teaspoon freshly cracked white or black pepper

sea salt

Serves 4

Combine the apples, pears, radicchio, spinach, and blue cheese in a large salad bowl and toss gently to combine.

Whisk the olive oil, tarragon vinegar, and pepper in a small bowl and season with a little salt. Pour the dressing over the salad, toss well, and serve immediately.

cauliflower and Swiss chard salad

If you've never tried a cauliflower salad, do try this recipe. Cauliflower has a firm, crunchy texture and creamy flavor which makes it perfect for this light and spicy dish with Middle Eastern-style flavorings. It makes a great winter buffet dish and is the perfect accompaniment to a Baked and Glazed Ham (see page 97) and cold leftover turkey.

Put the oil in a skillet and set over high heat. Add the cauliflower florets and cook for 8–10 minutes, turning often, until they are a dark, golden brown. Add the cumin and cook, stirring, for 1 minute. Add the Swiss chard, onion, and garlic to the pan and cook for a further 2–3 minutes. Add the chickpeas and stir. Season to taste with salt.

Combine the tahini, lemon juice, and white pepper in a small bowl and add a little salt to taste. Whisk to combine. Transfer the vegetables to a bowl and drizzle the dressing over the top to serve.

¼ cup light olive oil

1 small head of cauliflower, separated into large florets

1 teaspoon ground cumin

6 large Swiss chard leaves, chopped into 1-inch wide strips

1 red onion, cut into wedges

2 garlic cloves, chopped

14-oz. can chickpeas, rinsed and drained

¼ cup tahini (sesame seed paste)

2 tablespoons freshly squeezed lemon juice

¼ teaspoon freshly cracked white pepper

sea salt

Serves 4

chickpea salad with onions and paprika

1½ cups dried chickpeas, soaked in plenty of cold water overnight

1 red onion, cut in half lengthwise, then in half crosswise, and sliced with the grain

4 garlic cloves, finely chopped

1 teaspoon ground cumin

1–2 teaspoons paprika

3 tablespoons olive oil

freshly squeezed juice of 1 lemon

a small bunch of flatleaf parsley, coarsely chopped

a small bunch of cilantro, coarsely chopped

5 oz. firm goat cheese or feta, crumbled (optional)

sea salt and freshly ground black pepper

crusty bread, to serve

Serves 4

This hearty Moroccan salad is packed with filling legumes and is particularly good served warm, topped with crumbled goat cheese. If you don't have time to soak the chickpeas, you can use cooked tinned ones instead, but their texture won't be quite as good.

Drain the chickpeas and put them in a large saucepan. Cover with water and bring to a boil. Reduce the heat and simmer for about 45 minutes, until the chickpeas are tender but not mushy. Drain the chickpeas well and remove any loose skins—you can rub them in a clean kitchen towel or between your fingertips.

Tip them into a large bowl. Add the onion, garlic, cumin, paprika, olive oil, and lemon juice while the chickpeas are still warm.

Toss well, making sure the chickpeas are well coated. Season to taste and toss in most of the herbs. Crumble over the goat cheese, if using, and sprinkle with the rest of the herbs. Serve while still warm with plenty of crusty bread.

spiced tomato and lentil salad

This salad is from Lebanon and Syria, but similar lentil dishes can be found all round the eastern Mediterranean, from Egypt to Turkey. Sumac is a very popular Middle Eastern spice, enjoyed for its sour, almost lemony flavor. Use Umbrian lentils which, although not Middle Eastern, hold their texture well and are particularly flavorful.

1 cup brown lentils

5 tablespoons extra virgin olive oil

1 onion, halved and thinly sliced

1 basket cherry tomatoes, quartered

2 teaspoons sumac*, plus extra to serve

sea salt and freshly ground black pepper

Serves 4–6

Put the lentils into a large bowl, cover with plenty of cold water, and soak for 2 hours or according to the package instructions. Drain, transfer to a saucepan, add a pinch of salt, and cover with boiling water. Return

to a boil, reduce the heat, and simmer for about 15 minutes, until tender but still firm. Drain well and set aside.

Clean the saucepan, add 2 tablespoons of the oil, heat well, then add the onion. Fry gently for about 8 minutes until softened and translucent. Remove from the heat and add the lentils, tomatoes, sumac, salt, pepper, and the remaining oil. Stir gently with a wooden spoon and serve as a side dish, with extra sumac served separately.

*Note If you can't find sumac but would like to try this salad, opt for a completely different, but still Middle Eastern flavor. In the Levant, caraway is used in many ways, and will give this salad a light anise flavor rather than the sour edge provided by the sumac. Add 1 teaspoon caraway seeds when you heat the oil, then proceed with the recipe—a refreshing alternative.

roasted butternut squash and pancetta salad
with pumpkin oil and spiced dressing

This combination of roasted squash with a spicy dressing is a knockout. The recipe call for the type of apple pie spice usually saved for bakes but which is a well-balanced mixture of cassia, ginger, nutmeg, caraway, cloves, and coriander—not to be confused with Jamaican allspice, which is something very different.

1 large butternut squash, peeled

2 garlic cloves, peeled and crushed

1 teaspoon sugar

2 tablespoons pumpkin oil

6 oz. pancetta lardons or chopped bacon

a handful of arugula, to serve

sea salt and freshly ground black pepper

dressing

6 tablespoons pumpkin oil

2 tablespoons red wine vinegar

1–2 tablespoons runny honey

½ teaspoon apple pie spice

Serves 4

Preheat the oven to 400°F.

Seed the butternut squash and pop the seeds into a strainer. Wash them under cold running water until clean, then pat dry with paper towels.

Cut the squash flesh into bite-size chunks. Put in a roasting pan with the seeds and garlic, sprinkle with the sugar, and drizzle with the pumpkin oil. Season and toss well. Roast in the preheated oven for 10 minutes. Remove from the oven, scatter the pancetta lardons on top, and return to the oven for a further 15 minutes, or until the squash and garlic are soft and golden and the pancetta is crisp.

To make the dressing, put the pumpkin oil, red wine vinegar, honey, and apple pie spice in a saucepan, whisk to combine, and heat gently over low heat. Season to taste.

Put the roasted squash mixture on serving plates, drizzle with the warm dressing, and top each serving with a small handful of arugula. Serve immediately.

bakes and desserts

ginger and cinnamon thins

It's easy enough to buy spiced cookies, but it's worth baking them yourself if only for the gorgeous smell that permeates the kitchen. As well as being a welcome teatime treat, these pretty cookies make a lovely and inexpensive gift. Simply package in a pretty box and tie with ribbon.

½ cup dark brown sugar

1 stick unsalted butter, cut into cubes

6 tablespoons golden or corn syrup

6 tablespoons heavy cream

3 cups plus 2 tablespoons all-purpose flour

1 tablespoon ground ginger

1 tablespoon ground cinnamon

⅛ teaspoon ground cloves (optional)

1 teaspoon baking powder

½ teaspoon salt

2 baking sheets lined with baking parchment

star-shaped cookie cutters in various sizes (or any other shapes you like, such as Christmas trees, bells, angels, etc.)

Makes about 40 cookies

Sift the sugar through a coarse strainer to remove any lumps and put in a large bowl with the cubed butter. Beat together until smooth, then beat in the golden syrup and cream. Measure out the flour and add the ginger, cinnamon, cloves, baking powder, and salt and sift into another bowl. Add the flour and spice mixture to the creamed mixture a third at a time until you have a stiff dough. Form the dough into a flat disk, wrap in foil, and refrigerate for 3 hours.

When you're ready to bake the cookies preheat the oven to 375°F. Cut off a quarter of the dough, flour the work surface and rolling pin generously, and roll out the dough thinly. Stamp out shapes with your cutters. Carefully prise them off the work surface with a palate knife, lay them on one of the baking sheets, and bake in the preheated oven for about 8 minutes. Leave them to firm up for 2–3 minutes, then transfer to a wire rack until crisp. Repeat with the remaining pieces of dough, re-rolling the offcuts to give you as many cookies as possible. The cookies will keep in an airtight container for up to one week.

snowy pine nut cookies

1 stick plus 5 tablespoons unsalted butter, softened

½ cup superfine sugar

1½ cups all-purpose flour

½ teaspoon fine sea salt

1¼ cups pine nuts, roughly chopped

1 teaspoon pure almond extract

confectioners' sugar, to dust

2 baking sheets, lined with baking parchment

Makes about 20

Rich, buttery, and addictive, these delicious little cookies are dusted with confectioners' sugar while warm and again when cold. Serve with dessert wines, liqueurs, or spicy mulled wine.

Preheat the oven to 350°F.

Put the butter and superfine sugar in a large bowl and beat together until soft. Add the flour, salt, pine nuts, and almond extract and mix well to combine. Using your hands, form the mixture into about 20 small balls (about 1½ inches diameter) and place them slightly apart on the prepared baking sheets as they will spread during baking. Bake in the preheated oven for 12–15 minutes.

Let cool a little before transferring to a wire rack and dust with confectioners' sugar. Dust again when the cookies are cold. The cookies will keep in an airtight container for up to one week

stem ginger cookies

6 tablespoons unsalted butter, at room temperature

generous ⅓ cup raw sugar

1 egg yolk

½ teaspoon ground ginger

2 oz. stem ginger in syrup, chopped

¼ cup ground almonds

¾ cup self-rising flour

2 baking sheets, lined with baking parchment

Makes about 10

Preheat the oven to 325°F.

Beat the butter and sugar together until pale and creamy, then beat in the egg yolk. Stir in the ground ginger and stem ginger, then the ground almonds. Add the flour and mix well.

Roll the mixture into 10 walnut-size balls and arrange them on the prepared baking sheets, spacing well apart. Flatten slightly with your fingers and bake in the preheated oven for about 20 minutes, until a pale golden brown.

Let the cookies cool on the baking sheets for a few minutes. When firm, use a spatula to transfer them to a wire rack to cool. The cookies will keep in an airtight container for up to one week.

The spicy and chewy pieces of stem ginger give a flavor kick to these buttery, melt-in-the-mouth cookies. Served with a pot of warming lapsang souchong, they are the perfect addition to a cozy fireside tea.

iced star cookies

These cookies are simple to make and are ideal decorations. Pick your favorite novelty cookie cutters, then once they are baked, have fun icing and finishing.

Cream the butter with the sugar and grated lemon peel. Beat in 2 teaspoons of the lemon juice and the cream cheese. Sift in the flour, mixed spice, and salt and mix. When thoroughly combined, remove the dough from the bowl, shape into a ball, and wrap in plastic wrap. Chill until firm, about 30 minutes. The dough can be kept in the fridge, for up to 1 week.

When you're ready to bake the cookies preheat the oven to 350°F.

Remove the dough from the fridge and roll out on a lightly floured work surface until ¼ inch thick. Dip the cookie cutter in flour and cut out shapes. Gather up the trimmings and re-roll, then cut out more shapes. Arrange slightly apart on the baking sheets. If using as decorations, use a toothpick to make a small hole at the top of each shape large enough to thread a ribbon through. Bake in the preheated oven for about 12–15 minutes until just turning golden brown at the edges. Remove from the oven, let cool for 3 minutes, then transfer to a wire rack until completely cold. Decorate with glacé icing (see below), or use a writing icing pen. When firm, thread with ribbons. The cookies will keep in an airtight container for up to 5 days.

Glacé icing – Made with confectioners' sugar and water, plus a little coloring if you like, this icing will dry firm but not as hard as royal icing. Sift ¾ cup confectioners' sugar into a bowl. Stir in water or lemon juice, a teaspoon at a time, to make a thick icing that can be piped.

1¼ sticks unsalted butter, at room temperature

½ cup superfine sugar

finely grated peel and freshly squeezed juice of 1 lemon

⅛ cup cream cheese

2¼ cups all-purpose flour

1 teaspoon apple pie spice

a good pinch of salt

to decorate

glacé icing or writing icing pens, edible silver balls, twine, or ribbons

a star-shaped cookie cutter
several baking sheets

Makes about 24

cranberry and cherry florentines

These have to be the easiest cookies in the world to make, but they look impressive and taste delicious.

6 tablespoons unsalted butter

½ cup sugar

2 teaspoons clear honey

½ cup blanched almonds

⅔ cup mixed sun-dried cranberries, cherries, and blueberries

¾ cup all-purpose flour

5 oz. good-quality bittersweet chocolate (minimum 70% cocoa solids), broken into pieces

2–3 non-stick baking sheets or baking sheets lined with non-stick baking parchment

Makes 20–24

Preheat the oven to 350°F.

Put the butter, sugar, and honey in a saucepan and set over low heat. When the sugar has dissolved, bring almost to a boil, then take the pan off the heat. Stir in the almonds and fruit, then tip in the flour and mix thoroughly. Spoon heaping teaspoonfuls of the mixture onto the baking sheets, leaving plenty of space between each one. Flatten them slightly with the back of your spoon. Bake in the preheated oven for 10–12 minutes until the florentines have spread and are turning brown at the edges. Let cool for about 3 minutes, then prise them off the baking sheets and transfer to a wire rack. When they are completely cold, put the chocolate in a heatproof bowl and melt over a pan of barely simmering water, taking care that the bowl doesn't touch the water. Lay the florentines flat-side upwards on a sheet of baking parchment and spread the chocolate over them with a flat-bladed knife. Let them sit until the chocolate sets, then store in an airtight tin for up to 5 days.

---

1 stick unsalted butter, at room temperature

1 scant cup sugar

1 egg

1 tablespoon instant coffee granules dissolved in 1½ tablespoons just-boiled water

¾ cup macadamia nuts

¾ cup white chocolate, roughly chopped

⅔ cup self-rising flour

⅔ all-purpose flour

2 baking sheets, greased

Makes about 15

coffee, macadamia, and white chocolate chunk cookies

These big, fat, chunky, chewy cookies are subtly flavored with coffee and studded with chunks of white chocolate and macadamia nuts.

Preheat the oven to 375°F.

Cream together the butter and sugar until soft, then beat in the egg, followed by the coffee. Stir in the macadamia nuts and chocolate and mix together. Combine the flours and sift over the cookie mixture, then stir until thoroughly combined.

Drop heaping tablespoonfuls of the mixture on to the baking sheets, spacing them well apart. Bake for about 10 minutes until pale golden and slightly puffed up.

Let the cookies firm up for a few minutes, then transfer to a wire rack to cool. The cookies will keep in an airtight container for up to 3 days.

toasted teacakes

There's something comforting and homey about a plateful of freshly toasted teacakes dripping with butter, and the wonderful smell of spices that they emit. If you've got an old-fashioned toasting fork with a long handle, why not toast the teacakes the traditional way over the open fire?

1½ cups bread flour

½ teaspoon sea salt

1 teaspoon quick-rising active dry yeast

1½ tablespoons brown sugar

¼ teaspoon freshly grated nutmeg

⅓ cup mixed dried vine fruits

3 tablespoons butter, melted

½ cup full-fat milk, plus extra for brushing

butter, to serve

Makes 8

Sift the flour, salt, yeast, sugar, and nutmeg into a large bowl. Stir in the dried fruits and make a well in the center.

Put the milk and butter in a small saucepan and heat until just warm. Pour into the flour mixture and work together to make a soft dough. Turn out on to a lightly floured work surface and knead for about 5 minutes, until smooth and elastic. Place in a bowl, slip the bowl into a large plastic bag, seal and leave to rise for 1 hour, until doubled in size. When risen, tip the dough out on to a lightly floured work surface, punch down, and divide into eight pieces of equal size. Shape each one into a ball, flatten slightly and arrange on a non-stick baking sheet, spacing slightly apart. Slip the baking sheet into a plastic bag and leave the dough to rise for 45 minutes, until doubled in size.

Preheat the oven to 400°F.

Brush the top of each teacake with milk and bake in the preheated oven for about 15 minutes, until risen and golden. Transfer to a wire rack to cool. When ready to serve, split, toast on the cut sides, and spread generously with butter.

triple chocolate brownies

There are no nuts but plenty of rich chocolate in these moist brownies.

7 oz. dark bittersweet chocolate, chopped

7 tablespoons unsalted butter, at room temperature, cut into cubes

1 cup plus 2 tablespoons sugar

½ teaspoon real vanilla extract

4 eggs, at room temperature

½ cup all-purpose flour

⅔ cup unsweetened cocoa powder

4 oz. white chocolate, coarsely chopped

a baking pan, about 10 x 8 inches, greased and baselined with baking parchment

Makes 24

Preheat the oven to 350°F.

Melt the chocolate in a heatproof bowl set over a pan of simmering, but not boiling, water. Do not let the base of the bowl touch the water. Stir occasionally until melted, then remove the bowl from the heat and leave to cool until needed.

Beat the butter, sugar, and vanilla extract until light and fluffy, then gradually beat in the eggs, beating well after each addition.

Stir in the melted chocolate, then sift the flour and cocoa into the bowl and mix in. Transfer the mixture to the prepared pan and spread evenly. Scatter the chopped white chocolate over the top, then bake in the preheated oven for 20 minutes, or until a skewer inserted halfway between the sides and the center comes out slightly moist but not sticky with uncooked batter.

Remove the pan from the oven and set on a wire rack. Leave to cool completely, then cut into 24 pieces. Store in an airtight container and eat within 4 days.

crumpets

Homemade crumpets are even more wonderful than the store-bought kind. Fresh yeast gives the best result—it's often available to buy in small bakers or in-store supermarket bakeries—but if you can't find it, just use quick-rising active dry yeast instead.

1¼ cups full-fat milk mixed with 1¼ cups water

½ oz. compressed yeast or a ¼-oz package of quick-rising active dry yeast

3 cups all-purpose flour

½ teaspoon baking soda

1 teaspoon salt

to serve

unsalted butter

raspberry or strawberry jelly or honey

2–3 crumpet rings or scone cutters

a flat griddle pan or skillet, preheated and greased

Makes 12

Warm the milk and water mixture in a small saucepan. If using fresh yeast, put it into a small bowl with a little of the warm liquid, stir well, then add the remaining milk and water. Sift the flour into a mixing bowl, then stir in the warm yeast mixture. If you are using quick-rising active dry yeast, follow the manufacturer's instructions.

Cover the bowl with a clean kitchen towel and leave in a warm place for 1 hour. Put the baking soda and salt into a bowl, add 2 tablespoons water, mix well, then beat it into the mixture. Set aside for a further 45 minutes.

Put the greased crumpet rings on the prepared griddle pan and set over medium heat. When the rings are hot, spoon 2 tablespoons of the batter into each ring—just enough to cover the base. Let cook for about 4–5 minutes, until the underside is golden, then remove the rings and turn the crumpet over to brown the top.

To serve, toast the crumpets on both sides, spread them with butter, and stack on a hot plate. Serve with fruit jelly or honey.

gingerbread mini-muffins

Spicy, sticky, and utterly irresistible, these cute little muffins are always popular with children.

7 tablespoons unsalted butter

2 tablespoons molasses

2 tablespoons runny honey

⅔ cup firmly packed dark brown sugar

½ cup milk

1¼ cups all-purpose flour

1 teaspoon baking soda

1 tablespoon ground ginger

1 teaspoon ground cinnamon

a good pinch of salt

1 egg, beaten

2 oz. stem ginger, drained and finely chopped

glacé icing (see page 126), or writing icing pens

3 mini-muffin pans lined with mini-muffin cases, or use double cases set on a baking sheet

Makes about 36

Preheat the oven to 350°F.

Put the butter, molasses, honey, sugar, and milk in a saucepan over low heat and melt gently. Remove from the heat and leave to cool for a couple of minutes.

Sift the flour, baking soda, ground ginger, cinnamon, and salt into a mixing bowl. Pour in the cooled, melted mixture, then the egg. Mix thoroughly with a wooden spoon. Mix in the stem ginger.

Spoon the mixture into the cases. Bake in the preheated oven for about 15 minutes, until firm to the touch.

Leave to cool on a wire rack, then decorate with glacé icing. Store in an airtight container and eat within 3 days.

Christmas mini-muffins

1¼ cups all-purpose flour

1 teaspoon baking powder

a pinch of salt

¼ cup sugar

finely grated peel of ½ an orange

½ cup pecan pieces, coarsely chopped, plus 2 tablespoons extra, to decorate

1½ tablespoons raisins or golden raisins

½ cup fresh or frozen cranberries (no need to thaw)

1 egg, beaten

½ stick unsalted butter, melted

½ cup full-fat milk

confectioners' sugar, to dust

3 mini-muffin pans lined with mini-muffin cases, or use double cases set on a baking sheet

Makes about 36

Not as sweet as some muffins, these are perfect for brunch and breakfast along with a cup of good coffee.

Preheat the oven to 350°F.

Sift the flour, baking powder, and salt into a mixing bowl. Stir in the sugar, grated orange peel, chopped pecans, and raisins.

Put the cranberries into the bowl of a food processor and chop roughly. Stir them into the flour mixture. Combine the beaten egg with the melted butter and milk and stir into the flour mixture with a wooden spoon.

Spoon the mixture into the cases using 2 teaspoons, then decorate with the extra pecans. Bake in the preheated oven for 12–15 minutes until golden and firm to the touch.

Turn out onto a wire rack. Serve warm, dusted with confectioners' sugar. Store in an airtight container and eat within 2 days.

sticky marzipan and cherry loaf

Studded with sweet candied cherries and with a surprise layer of marzipan running through the center, this simple loaf cake will become a firm favorite.

1½ sticks butter, at room temperature

¾ cups sugar

3 eggs

generous 1 cup self-rising flour

scant 1 cup ground almonds

6 oz. candied cherries, halved

3 oz. chilled marzipan, finely grated

confectioners' sugar, to dust

a 9 x 5 x 3-inch loaf pan, greased and lined

Serves 8–12

Preheat the oven to 350°F.

Put the butter and sugar in a large bowl and beat until pale and creamy. Beat in the eggs one at a time. Sift in the flour and fold in, then stir in the cherries.

Spoon half the mixture into the prepared loaf pan and level the surface. Sprinkle with the grated marzipan. Top with the remaining mixture and smooth the surface.

Bake in the preheated oven for about 45 minutes, then remove the cake from the oven and cover the top with foil. Return it to the oven and bake for a further 25 minutes, until risen and golden and a skewer inserted in the center comes out clean. Leave to cool in the pan for about 10 minutes, then transfer to a wire rack to cool. Serve the cake at room temperature.

chocolate brandy cake

A rich chocolate treat to serve in thin slices with coffee or whipped cream for dessert. There's no baking involved as it's made from melting very good bitter chocolate with butter, then mixing with whisked eggs and sugar and flavoring with brandy (or walnut liqueur if you can find it), toasted walnuts, and the best dried cranberries you can find.

9 oz. good quality dark bittersweet chocolate (minimum 70% cocoa solids), coarsely chopped

2 sticks unsalted butter, diced

9 oz. graham crackers or wheaten cookies

2 eggs, at room temperature

4 tablespoons sugar

1⅔ cups walnut halves, lightly toasted

¾ cup ready-to-eat, soft-dried cranberries

4 tablespoons brandy or walnut liqueur

unsweetened cocoa powder, to dust

a springform cake pan, lined with plastic wrap

Serves 16

Melt the chocolate and butter in a heatproof bowl set over a pan of steaming but not boiling water. Do not let the base of the bowl touch the water. Stir frequently until melted, then remove the bowl from the heat and leave to cool until needed. Coarsely crush the cookies with a rolling pin or in a food processor.

Using an electric or rotary whisk, beat the eggs with the sugar until very thick and mousse-like and the whisk leaves a ribbon-like trail when lifted out of the bowl. Whisk in the melted chocolate mixture.

Coarsely chop two-thirds of the walnuts and carefully fold in with the cranberries, brandy and crushed cookies.

Spoon into the prepared pan and spread evenly. Decorate with the rest of the walnut halves. Cover the top of the pan with plastic wrap and chill for at least 4 hours.

When ready to serve, unclip the pan and remove the plastic wrap. Dust with cocoa and serve cut into slices. Store in an airtight container in the fridge for up to 1 week.

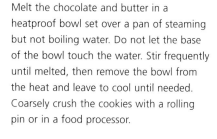

Swedish saffron cake

This deliciously rich, golden-hued cake uses saffron for the flavor and color. Serve with whipped cream and a dollop of any red fruit jelly on the side.

½ cup full-fat milk

2 sticks slightly salted butter

1 teaspoon saffron threads

2 eggs, at room temperature

1 cup raw sugar

1⅔ cups all-purpose flour

2 teaspoons baking powder

confectioners' sugar, to dust

a 9-inch springform cake pan, greased, baselined with baking parchment and sprinkled with dried bread crumbs or ground almonds

Serves 8–12

Pour the milk into a saucepan. Add the butter and heat until melted and steaming hot but not at a boil. Remove the pan from the heat and sprinkle in the saffron. Cover and leave to infuse for 1 hour.

When ready to bake the cake, preheat the oven to 350°F.

Put the eggs in a mixing bowl and whisk until just frothy. Whisk in the sugar and continue whisking until the mixture is very thick and mousse-like and the whisk leaves a trail when lifted out of the bowl.

Gently fold in the just-warm saffron mixture. Sift the flour and baking powder into the bowl and fold in gently with a large metal spoon—the mixture will look hopeless at first but it will combine after a minute.

Pour into the prepared pan and bake in the preheated oven for 35–40 minutes until the cake is a good golden brown, slightly shrunk from the sides of the pan, and firm to the touch. Put on a wire rack and unclip the pan. Leave to cool completely then serve dusted with confectioners' sugar. Store in an airtight container and eat within 4 days.

1½ sticks unsalted butter, at room temperature

generous ¾ cup sugar

3 eggs

generous 1 cup self-rising flour

2 teaspoons instant coffee granules, dissolved in 1 tablespoon hot water

½ cup walnut pieces

coffee frosting

9 oz. mascarpone cheese

½ cup confectioners' sugar, sifted

1½ teaspoons instant coffee granules, dissolved in 2 teaspoons hot water

walnut halves, to decorate

2 x 8-inch diameter round cake pans, greased and baselined with baking parchment

Serves 8–12

coffee and walnut cake

This classic teatime cake is enduringly popular, perhaps because something magical happens when coffee and walnuts come together.

Preheat the oven to 350°F.

Put the butter and sugar in a mixing bowl and cream together until pale and fluffy. Beat in the eggs one at a time. Sift the flour into the butter mixture and stir to combine. Fold in the walnuts and coffee. Divide the cake mixture between the prepared pans and level out the surface of each.

Bake in the preheated oven for 20–25 minutes until golden and a skewer inserted in the center of the cake comes out clean.

Transfer to a wire rack, carefully peel off the baking parchment, and let cool completely before frosting.

To make the frosting, beat together the mascarpone, confectioners' sugar, and coffee until smooth and creamy. Spread slightly less than half of the frosting over one of the cooled cakes, then place the second cake on top. Spread the remaining frosting over the top and decorate with walnut halves. Store in an airtight container and eat within 2 days.

pear and ginger crumble cake

This is a deliciously spicy cake with an interesting texture. Note that ground ginger loses its intensity if left sitting in the pantry for too long, so do make sure that what you use here is not past it's use-by date. You can also follow this recipe substituting apples for the pears. If you decide to try it that way, use ground cinnamon instead of the ginger.

1 stick unsalted butter, softened

½ cup plus 2 tablespoons sugar

2 eggs, at room temperature

1 cup all-purpose flour

2 teaspoons baking powder

2 firm pears, peeled, cored, and sliced

1 tablespoon freshly squeezed lemon juice

heavy cream, to serve (optional)

ginger crumble

½ cup all-purpose flour

1 teaspoon ground ginger

3 tablespoons light brown sugar

3 tablespoons chilled unsalted butter, cubed

a 9-inch diameter springform cake pan, baselined with baking parchment and greased

Serves 6–8

To make the crumble mixture, put the flour and ginger in a mixing bowl. Add the chilled butter and quickly rub it into the flour using your fingertips. Add the sugar and rub again until the mixture resembles coarse sand. Refrigerate until needed.

Preheat the oven to 350°F.

Beat the softened butter and sugar until pale and creamy. Add the eggs, 1 at a time, and beat well between each addition. Tip in the flour and baking powder and beat for 1 minute, until the mixture is smooth and well combined. Pour it into the prepared pan. Toss the pears in a bowl with the lemon juice and put them on top of the cake. Sprinkle the crumble topping over the top and bake in the preheated oven for 40–45 minutes until the cake is golden.

Let cool slightly before removing from the pan and serving warm with heavy cream, if liked. Store in an airtight container and eat within 2–3 days.

pear and almond tart

This is elegant, both in appearance and flavor. It is ideal for entertaining since the tart shell and almond cream can be made a few hours in advance. Serve with sweetened crème fraîche, or good quality vanilla ice cream.

3–4 ripe pears

7 tablespoons unsalted butter

½ cup sugar

2 eggs

½ cup ground almonds

2 tablespoons all-purpose flour

pastry

1½ cups all-purpose flour, plus extra for rolling

2 teaspoons sugar

7 tablespoons cold unsalted butter, cut into cubes

a pinch of salt

baking parchment and baking weights or beans

an 11-inch diameter loosebased tart pan, greased and floured

Serves 6

To make the pastry, put the flour, sugar, butter, and salt in a food processor and, using the pulse button, process until the butter is broken down (about 5–10 pulses.) Add 3 tablespoons cold water and pulse until the mixture forms coarse crumbs; add 1 more tablespoon if necessary but do not do more than 10 pulses.

Transfer the pastry to a sheet of baking parchment, form into a ball, and flatten to a disk. Wrap in paper and let sit for 30–60 minutes.

Roll out the pastry on a floured work surface to a disk slightly larger than the tart pan. Carefully transfer the pastry to the pan, patching any holes as you go and pressing gently into the sides. To trim the edges, roll a rolling pin over the top, using the edge of the pan as a cutting surface, and letting the excess fall away. Tidy up the edges and chill until firm, about 40 minutes.

Preheat the oven to 400°F. Prick the pastry all over, line with baking parchment, and fill with baking weights. Bake on a low shelf in the preheated oven for 15 minutes, then remove the paper and weights and bake until just golden, 10–15 minutes more. Let the tart shell cool slightly before filling.

To make the almond cream, put the butter and sugar in a bowl and beat with an electric mixer until fluffy. Beat in the eggs, 1 at a time. Using a spatula, fold in the almonds and flour until well mixed.

Lower the oven temperature to 375°F. Spread the almond cream evenly in the tart shell.

Peel and slice the pears, into 8 or 12 slices, depending on the size of the pears. Arrange the slices on top of the almond cream. Bake in the preheated oven until puffed and golden, about 20–25 minutes. Serve warm.

sticky date flaky tarts with caramel oranges

Fresh dates are so sweet and sticky, they make a fantastic quick-and-easy topping for a crisp puff pastry base. The maple syrup and sugar caramelize with the butter and give the tarts a wonderful sheen. Don't serve them too hot, or you will burn your mouth.

1 sheet of ready-rolled puff pastry dough, defrosted if frozen

caramel oranges

4 small, juicy, thin-skinned oranges

½ cup plus 2 tablespoons sugar

date topping

6 tablespoons unsalted butter

3 tablespoons light brown sugar

2 tablespoons maple syrup

12–16 fresh Medjool dates

¼ cup walnut pieces

a 5-inch diameter saucer or similar (to use as a template)

Serves 4

Preheat the oven to 400°F.

Unroll the pastry on a lightly floured work surface. Cut out 4 circles, using the saucer as a template. Put these on a non-stick baking sheet, prick all over, then chill or freeze for 15 minutes.

Meanwhile, make the caramel oranges. Slice the top and bottom off of each orange, then cut off the skin in a spiral, as if you were peeling an apple. Try to remove all the bitter white pith. Slice down between the membranes and flick out each segment. Catch the juice in a bowl.

Put the sugar and 3 tablespoons water into a heavy-based saucepan. Set over low heat until the sugar has completely dissolved and the liquid is clear. Increase the heat and boil until the liquid turns a dark caramel color. Quickly remove the pan from the heat,

stand back and add another 3 tablespoons water—it will hiss and splutter.

Return the pan to a low heat, and stir until all the hardened pieces of caramel have dissolved. Pour in the reserved orange juice and boil hard until very thick and syrupy. Remove from the heat and let cool completely before adding the orange segments. Chill until needed.

To make the date topping, cut the dates in half and remove the pits. Put the butter, sugar, and maple syrup in a saucepan and melt over gentle heat, then add the dates and walnuts.

Spoon the mixture over the pastry circles, leaving a small clear rim on the outside of each. Bake in the preheated oven for 15–18 minutes until the pastry is risen and golden. Serve with the caramel oranges.

real treacle tart with caramelized bananas

Treacle tart is often made with golden syrup, white bread crumbs, and lemon juice but this fabulous recipe uses molasses, German rye bread (pumpernickel), and lime juice. The pumpernickel gives it an unusual, wonderful texture.

Preheat the oven to 375°F.

On a lightly floured work surface, roll out the pastry to a thickness of ⅛ inch. Use to line the pie plate and prick the base. Using a small sharp knife, make small cuts the width of the pastry edge about a thumb's breadth apart. Fold over every "flap" diagonally onto itself towards the center of the pan, pressing the tips, (not the folds) downwards to seal. Chill or freeze the pastry for 10–15 minutes.

Put the treacle and golden syrup in a large saucepan, add the lime juice and grated zest and ginger, if using, and heat until just warm and runny. Stir in the pumpernickel crumbs. Spread the mixture into the pastry

case and bake in the preheated oven for about 30 minutes, or until the filling is just set and the pastry is browning at the edges.

Meanwhile, peel the bananas and cut them into chunks. Melt the butter in a skillet and add the sugar. Cook for a couple of minutes until the sugar melts, then turn up the heat and cook until it caramelizes. Add the bananas, toss well to coat with the juices and sauté over medium heat until starting to color. Squeeze in some lemon juice, and remove from the heat.

Cool the tart slightly before serving warm with the caramelized bananas and ice cream, heavy cream, or crème fraîche on the side.

13-oz. ready-made shortcrust pastry dough

5 tablespoons molasses

5 tablespoons golden or corn syrup

finely grated peel and juice of 1 large lime

½ teaspoon freshly grated ginger
(optional but recommended)

4 oz. pumpernickel crumbs
(use a food processor to make the crumbs)

caramelized bananas

2 large bananas

6 tablespoons unsalted butter

3 tablespoons light brown sugar

a squeeze of fresh lemon juice

ice cream, heavy cream, or crème fraîche,
to serve

an 8-inch diameter shallow pie plate

Serves 4–6

individual caramelized pear and cranberry tarts

1 sheet of ready-rolled puff pastry dough, defrosted if frozen

2 large ripe pears, peeled, halved, and cored

1 oz. dried cranberries

2 tablespoons unsalted butter, chilled and cut into cubes

full-fat milk, to glaze

3 tablespoons granulated sugar or 3 oz. sugar cubes, crushed (see recipe introduction)

1 teaspoon cinnamon

light cream or sour cream, to serve

a non-stick baking sheet

Serves 4

Having a package of ready-rolled puff pastry dough in the freezer is a great standby for an instant fruit tart. You can use practically any fruit; peaches, nectarines, apricots, plums, apples, or blueberries. To crush sugar cubes, put them in a plastic bag and beat with the end of a rolling pin. They give a deliciously crunchy effect.

Preheat the oven to 425°F.

Lightly flour a work surface and unroll the pastry. Use a sharp knife or a pizza wheel to cut it into 4 squares of equal size. Place the pastry squares on a non-stick baking sheet.

Divide the dried cranberries between the pastry squares and place a pear half in the center of each one. Scatter with the cubed butter. Brush the edges with a little milk. Mix the sugar or crushed sugar cubes with the cinnamon and sprinkle over the top.

Carefully slide the tarts onto the hot baking sheet and return to the preheated oven to cook for about 35–40 minutes, until the pastry is golden brown and crisp and the pears are tender. Serve whilst still warm with light cream or sour cream.

13-oz. package of ready-made shortcrust pastry dough

vanilla ice cream or custard sauce, to serve

crumble topping

½ cup all-purpose flour

⅓ cup light brown sugar

6 tablespoons unsalted butter, softened

finely grated peel of 1 lemon

spiced apple filling

6 large apples, such as Cox's Orange Pippins or Granny Smith, peeled and cored

⅓ cup golden raisins

finely grated peel and juice of 1 lemon

¼ cup light brown sugar

½ teaspoon ground cinnamon

¼ teaspoon ground nutmeg

1 tablespoon each all-purpose flour and sugar, mixed together

a 9-inch diameter tart pan

baking parchment and baking weights or beans

Serves 6

lemony apple crumble tart

This family favorite is easy to make and children love the crumble topping.

Preheat the oven to 400°F.

On a lightly floured work surface, roll out the pastry to a thickness of ¼ inch. Use to line the tart pan. Prick the base, then chill or freeze for 15 minutes. Line with baking parchment and fill with baking weights. Put on a baking sheet and bake in the center of the oven for 10–12 minutes. Remove the baking parchment and the weights and return the pastry shell to the oven for a further 5–7 minutes. Let cool.

To make the crumble topping, put the flour, sugar, butter, and grated lemon peel in a bowl and rub lightly between your fingers until the mixture resembles fine bread crumbs. To make the apple filling, chop the apples into small chunks, put into a bowl and toss with the golden raisins, grated lemon peel and juice, sugar, and spices. Sprinkle the base of the pastry shell with the flour and sugar, then arrange the apples on top. Sprinkle the crumble mixture over the apples. Bake in the preheated oven for 15 minutes, then reduce the temperature to 350°F and bake for another 30 minutes. Serve warm with vanilla ice cream or custard sauce.

apple and blueberry tarts

These are a cheat's delight—so simple and quick to make and deliciously fresh-tasting. Use Red Delicious apples in fall at a time when blueberries are in their last few weeks. Both fruits are perfect to cook with and just lovely with the vanilla. Any leftover tarts can be served cold and enjoyed with coffee the next day. Just dust them with some confectioners' sugar and eat them as you would a fruit-filled Danish.

1 sheet of ready-rolled puff pastry dough, defrosted if frozen

2 tablespoons sugar

1 vanilla bean, split in half lengthwise

3 sweet dessert apples (such as Red Delicious or Braeburn), each cored and cut into 10–12 thin wedges

1 basket of blueberries (about 6 oz.)

heavy cream, to serve

Serves 4

Preheat the oven to 425°F.

Lightly flour a work surface and unroll the pastry. Use a sharp knife or a pizza wheel to cut it into 4 squares of equal size. Place the pastry squares on a non-stick baking sheet.

Put the sugar and 2 tablespoons of water in a saucepan and bring to a boil, stirring until the sugar dissolves. Scrape the seeds from the vanilla bean directly into the sugar syrup, stirring to combine.

Add the apple slices to the pan, reduce the heat to medium and cook for 4–5 minutes, turning the apples so they cook evenly. Add the blueberries and gently stir to coat in the sweet syrup. Arrange the apples and blueberries on top of each pastry square. Bake in the preheated oven for 18–20 minutes, until the pastry is puffed and golden.

Serve warm with cream spooned over the top.

Variation: For a simple French-style apple frangipane tart, mix 2 tablespoons each of room temperature butter, ground almonds, and confectioners' sugar with 1 tablespoon all-purpose flour in a bowl until you have a paste. Stir in 1 egg yolk until smooth. Spread the mixture over each of the pastry squares, leaving a space around the edge, and top with the apple slices. Bake in a preheated oven at 425°F for 18–20 minutes, until puffed and golden.

baked plums in puff pastry
with crème fraîche

Make this quick and easy yet elegant dessert with whatever fruit is in season, such as apples, pears, apricots, or plums, as used here. Be sure to use just-soft plums, not too ripe. You can prepare the fruit and pastries in advance and assemble just before serving. If necessary, reheat the plums slightly as they are best served warm. How you shape the pastries is up to you—rectangles, squares, triangles, or circles all work fine!

1 sheet of ready-rolled puff pastry dough, defrosted if frozen

1 egg, beaten

sugar, for the pastry

6–8 large red plums (not ripe), halved, pitted, and quartered

¼ cup sugar

1 cup crème fraîche or sour cream, sweetened with 1–2 tablespoons sugar

a non-stick baking sheet

Serves 6

Preheat the oven to 425°F.

Lightly flour a work surface and unroll the pastry. Use a sharp knife or a pizza wheel to cut it into 6 rectangles of equal size. Place the pastry on a non-stick baking sheet.

Brush with the egg and sprinkle each rectangle very generously with sugar. Bake in the preheated oven until puffed and browned. Let cool.

Reduce the oven temperature to 375°F. Put the plums in a baking dish, sprinkle with the sugar, and bake for 20–30 minutes, until tender and slightly browned. Let cool. To serve, split the pastries in half, fill with the plums, and add a dollop of sweetened crème fraîche or sour cream.

roast pumpkin and pecan pie

This recipe may look slightly daunting, but it is worth the effort. Do oven roast the pumpkin if you're cooking it from scratch—it has a much better texture than when you boil it.

pastry

2 cups all-purpose flour

1 teaspoon ground ginger

2 tablespoons confectioners' sugar

1 stick butter, chilled and cut into cubes

2 tablespoons vegetable shortening

1 egg yolk (reserve the white)

a pinch of salt

pumpkin purée

1 lb. pumpkin flesh (see method)

1 tablespoon bourbon or dark rum

1 tablespoon light brown sugar

¼ teaspoon mixed spice

1 tablespoon butter, chilled

pie filling

½ cup light brown sugar

1 tablespoon maple syrup or clear honey

1½ teaspoons apple pie spice

½ teaspoon ground cinnamon

a pinch of salt

1 tablespoon bourbon or dark rum

3 eggs

2 tablespoons all-purpose flour, sifted

⅔ cup heavy cream

topping

⅓ cup pecan nuts

1 tablespoon light brown sugar

lightly whipped cream, to serve

a 9-inch diameter fluted tart pan

baking weights or dried beans

Serves 6

To make the pastry, sift the flour, ginger, and confectioners' sugar into a mixing bowl. Cut the butter and shortening into the flour, then rub lightly with your fingertips until the mixture resembles coarse bread crumbs. Mix the egg yolk with 2 tablespoons ice water, add to the bowl, mix lightly, and pull together into a ball, adding extra water if needed. Shape into a flat disk, put in a plastic bag, and refrigerate for at least 30 minutes.

Preheat the oven to 400°F.

To make the pumpkin purée, scrape away all the pumpkin seeds and fibrous flesh surrounding them and cut the flesh into even-size chunks. Put these on a piece of lightly oiled foil. Sprinkle over the bourbon, sugar, and apple pie spice and dot with the cold butter. Bring the foil up round the sides and fold over carefully to form a loose but airtight package. Place in a baking dish and cook in the preheated oven for 40 minutes until the pumpkin is soft. Carefully open up the foil, let cool for a few minutes, then tip the pumpkin and the juices into a food processor and whizz until smooth.

Roll out the pastry and lower it into the tart pan. Trim the edges and press the base well into the pan. Prick lightly with a fork and chill for another 30 minutes. Line the pastry shell with foil and fill with baking weights. Bake at 400°F for 12 minutes, then remove the foil and weights, brush the base of the pastry shell with the reserved egg white to seal it, and return to the oven for about 3–4 minutes. Remove it from the oven and lower the temperature to 375°F.

Add the sugar and maple syrup to the pumpkin purée, then the spices, salt, and bourbon. Add the eggs, one by one, beating them in well, then sift in the flour and mix lightly. Add the cream and pour the filling into the pie shell. Put the pan on a baking sheet and bake in the still-hot oven for about 50 minutes until the filling is just set and firm, reducing the temperature to 350°F after 25 minutes.

About 10 minutes before the end of the cooking time, chop the pecan nuts finely. Put them in a saucepan with the sugar and warm gently until the sugar starts to melt. About 5 minutes before the tart is cooked sprinkle the nuts evenly over the surface of the tart and return it to the oven for 5 minutes. Remove from the oven and let cool for 20 minutes before cutting. Serve warm with lightly whipped cream.

dusky apple pie

This rustic apple pie with its spiced crumbly pastry and lemon-infused apple filling is perfect winter comfort food and guaranteed to become a family favorite.

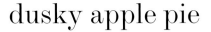

8 tart green apples (such as Granny Smith), peeled, cored, and thinly sliced

2 teaspoons freshly squeezed lemon juice

2 thin slices of lemon peel

¼ cup sugar

2 cups self-rising flour

¾ cup packed brown sugar

1 tablespoon ground cinnamon

1 tablespoon ground ginger

1 stick cold butter, cut into cubes

1 egg, lightly beaten

vanilla ice cream, to serve

a 9-inch diameter fluted pie plate, lightly greased

Serves 8–10

Put the apple slices in a saucepan with the lemon juice, lemon peel, and sugar. Cover and cook over low heat for 15–20 minutes, turning the apples often so they soften and cook evenly. Set aside and let cool.

To make the pastry, put the flour, brown sugar, and spices in a food processor and process for a few seconds to combine. With the motor running, add the butter several cubes at a time. Add the egg and 1–2 tablespoons of ice water and process until combined. The dough will look dry and crumbly. Transfer to a bowl and knead to form a ball. Wrap the ball in plastic wrap and refrigerate for 30 minutes.

Preheat the oven to 350°F and put a baking sheet in the oven to heat up. Cut the dough into two portions, with one slightly larger than the other. Roll the larger piece of

dough between two sheets of baking parchment and use it to line the bottom and sides of the prepared pie plate. (Take care when handling the pastry dough as it will be quite crumbly.) Trim the edge of the dough to fit the pan.

Spoon the apples on top of the pie shell. Roll the remaining pastry dough to a circle large enough to cover the pie and place on top, trimming the edges to fit. Use a small sharp knife to make several slits in the pastry. Put the pie on the hot baking sheet and bake in the preheated oven for 50–55 minutes, until the pastry is golden brown.

Remove the pie from the oven and let it rest for 15–20 minutes before cutting into wedges and serving with vanilla ice cream on the side.

gooseberry and ginger wine crumble

2 lbs. fresh or frozen gooseberries
or 2 x 12-oz. jars of gooseberries in juice,
well drained

3 tablespoons ginger wine

½ cup sugar

ginger topping

1½ cups all-purpose flour

1 teaspoon ground ginger

a pinch of salt

1 stick cold unsalted butter, cut into cubes

½ cup sugar

heavy cream or vanilla ice cream, to serve

a shallow ovenproof dish

Serves 4

Although gooseberries are a summer fruit they pair so perfectly with spicy ginger wine that it's worth freezing a batch in summer ready to bake this delicious crumble once the days start to get shorter. If fresh gooseberries aren't available, good-quality jarred fruit will work fine, but make sure you drain it well as too much liquid will make the crumble rather too soggy.

Preheat the oven to 375°F and put a baking sheet in the oven to heat.

Place the gooseberries in a nonmetal saucepan, add the ginger wine and sugar and cook gently until the fruit starts to burst. Remove from the heat and tip the gooseberries into a strainer set over a clean saucepan to catch the juices. Next tip the gooseberries into an ovenproof baking dish, covering the base with a single layer.

To make the crumble topping, put the flour, ginger, salt, and butter in a food processor and process until the mixture resembles coarse bread crumbs. (Alternatively you can rub in by hand.) Tip into a mixing bowl and stir in the sugar. (At this stage you can pop it into a plastic bag and chill in the fridge until ready to cook.)

Lightly sprinkle the topping mixture evenly over the prepared gooseberry mixture, mounding it up a little towards the center. Put the dish on the hot baking sheet and bake in the preheated oven for about 25 minutes, until crisp and golden. Let cool for 5 minutes before serving with and heavy cream or vanilla ice cream.

apple, prune, and armagnac phyllo crumble

There is a dessert in south-west France called Pastis Gascon, which is a buttery, apple or prune tart with a feather-light topping of sugar-dusted phyllo pastry, suffused with local fiery Armagnac. This recipe re-interprets it as a crumble.

4 sheets of ready-made phyllo pastry dough, defrosted if frozen

1 stick unsalted butter, melted

4 eating apples

16 ready-to-eat pitted prunes

2–3 tablespoons Armagnac or Cognac

3 tablespoons sugar

finely grated peel of 1 lemon

confectioners' sugar, to dust

light cream, to serve

a shallow ovenproof dish

Serves 4

Preheat the oven to 375°F.

Lay the phyllo dough out on a work surface and brush with the melted butter. Leave to set and dry out for 15–20 minutes.

Meanwhile, peel, core, and slice the apples and quarter the prunes. Toss them together in a bowl with the Armagnac, sugar, and the grated lemon peel. Pile the fruit into a baking dish, cover with foil, and bake in the preheated oven for 20 minutes.

Scrunch the pastry up so that it rips and tears and breaks into small rags. Remove the apple and prune mixture from the oven and lightly scatter the phyllo pieces on top, making sure it looks quite ragged and spiky. Dust lightly with confectioners' sugar and bake for a further 20 minutes, until golden.

Let cool for 5 minutes before serving with light cream for pouring.

mulled winter fruit crumble

Christmas is definitely coming when the smell of this delicious baked dessert starts to drift around the house. A mixture of either traditional or exotic dried fruits provides a rich base for the light crumbly topping. The spicy mulled wine seeps into the fruits as they cook and plumps them up nicely. Serve this with vanilla ice cream for a treat.

12 oz. mixed dried fruits such as golden raisins, cranberries, apricots, and figs or mango, pineapple, and paw-paw

1 generous cup medium-bodied fruity red wine

1 small cheesecloth bag of mulled wine spices (cinnamon, cloves, and allspice)

a thin strip of orange peel

¼ cup sugar

heavy cream or vanilla ice cream, to serve

spiced topping

1½ cups whole-wheat flour

¼ teaspoon mixed spice

a pinch of salt

1 stick cold unsalted butter, cut into cubes

½ cup light brown sugar

a shallow ovenproof dish

Serves 4

Preheat the oven to 375°F and put a baking sheet in the oven to heat.

Chop the dried fruits into bite-size pieces and place them in a nonmetal saucepan. Add the wine, mulling spices, orange peel, and sugar. Heat gently, then let simmer for 10 minutes. Let cool then spoon into an ovenproof dish and remove the mulling spices and orange peel.

To make the topping, put the flour, mixed spice, salt, and butter in a food processor and process until the mixture resembles coarse bread crumbs. (Alternatively you can rub in

by hand.) Tip the mixture into a bowl and stir in the sugar. (At this stage you can pop it into a plastic bag and chill in the fridge ready to cook.)

Lightly sprinkle the crumble topping mixture evenly over the surface of the dried fruits, mounding it up a little towards the center. Put the dish on the hot baking sheet and bake in the preheated oven for about 25 minutes, until crisp and golden on top.

Let cool for 5 minutes before serving with heavy cream or vanilla ice cream.

4–5 cooking apples, such as Bramley

2 cups fresh or frozen blackberries

4 tablespoons sugar

¼ teaspoon apple pie spice

finely grated peel and juice of ½ a lemon

crumble topping

1¾ sticks cold unsalted butter

1½ cups all-purpose flour

a pinch of salt

⅓ cup light brown sugar

light cream, to serve

a shallow, ovenproof dish

Serves 6

classic blackberry and apple crumble

Who can resist a classic fruit crumble warm from the oven. It is important to bake this traditional recipe in a moderate oven for a long time as this is what gives the topping its wonderful trademark crunch.

Preheat the oven to 350°F and put a baking sheet in the oven to heat.

Peel, core, and slice the apples and put them in a large bowl. Add the blackberries, sugar, apple pie spice, grated lemon peel, and juice and toss well to mix. Transfer to an ovenproof dish.

To make the crumble topping, rub the butter into the flour with the salt until the mixture resembles coarse bread crumbs. Alternatively do this in a food processor. Stir in the sugar. (At this stage the mixture can be popped into a plastic bag and chilled in the fridge until ready to cook.)

Lightly scatter the topping mixture over the fruit. Put the dish on the hot baking sheet and bake in the preheated oven for 50–60 minutes, until the golden and bubbling.

Remove from the oven and serve warm with light cream for pouring

plum and hazelnut pandowdy

A pandowdy is made with a sweet dough baked on top of fruit, the crust being "dowdied" by pushing the sweet dough into the fruit juices to soften it before serving. It can also be served upside down like a Tarte Tatin.

2 lbs. mixed plums, halved, pitted, and sliced

½ cup light brown sugar

½ teaspoon ground cinnamon

finely grated peel and juice of 1 small orange

3 tablespoons cold unsalted butter, cut into pieces

pandowdy crust

2 cups all-purpose flour

3 tablespoons sugar, plus extra to sprinkle

1 tablespoon baking powder

1 stick less 1 tablespoon cold unsalted butter, cut into pieces

3 oz. finely ground hazelnuts

1 cup light cream, plus extra to serve

an 11-inch diameter skillet, preferably cast-iron

Serves 6

Preheat the oven to 425°F. Put the plums in a bowl with the sugar, cinnamon, grated orange peel, and juice. Tip the fruit into the skillet and dot with the butter.

To make the pandowdy crust, sift the flour, sugar, and baking powder into a large bowl. Rub the cold butter into the flour until the mixture resembles coarse bread crumbs. Add the ground hazelnuts and mix. Stir in all but a couple of tablespoons of the cream with a blunt knife, until the dough comes together. It will be sticky. Knead very lightly until smooth. Working quickly, roll out to a circle ¼ inch thick and ½ inch wider than the pan. With the help of the rolling pin, lift the dough over the fruit and over the edge of the pan. Do not press the crust onto the sides of the pan. Make a couple of slits in the dough to allow steam to escape. Brush with the remaining cream and sprinkle with sugar.

Put the pan on a baking sheet to catch any leaking juices and bake in the preheated oven for 10 minutes, then reduce the oven temperature to 350°F and loosely cover with foil. Bake for a further 35–40 minutes, until the crust is golden. Remove from the oven and "dowdy" the crust by sharply pushing it under the surface of bubbling fruit with a large spoon. Serve warm with light cream for pouring.

baked Granny Smith and blueberry pudding

Granny Smith apples are a great all-round cooking apple. Their flesh collapses when cooked, making them perfect for applesauce but they are also great in sweet desserts, such as this self-saucing one, but they are not ideal for tarts and cakes. This recipe uses fresh blueberries which are now widely available throughout the year, but you could also use blackberries or cranberries.

2 tart green apples, such as Granny Smith

1 cup fresh blueberries

1 cup all-purpose flour

3 teaspoons baking powder

½ cup plus 2 tablespoons sugar

1 cup buttermilk

1 egg

1 vanilla bean

½ cup light brown sugar

light cream, to serve (optional)

a medium baking dish, well buttered

Serves 6

Preheat the oven to 350°F.

Peel and core the apples then thinly slice them directly into the prepared baking dish, arranging them in the bottom of the dish with the blueberries.

Sift the flour, baking powder, and sugar into a large bowl. Put the buttermilk and egg in a separate bowl. Split the vanilla bean in half lengthwise and scrape the seeds from the bean directly into this bowl, then stir to combine. Pour the buttermilk mixture into the flour mixture and beat well.

Pour the mixture over the fruit in the baking dish. Working quickly, put the brown sugar in a pitcher and add 1 cup boiling water. Stir until the sugar has dissolved. Carefully pour this mixture into the baking dish, pouring into a corner. Bake the pudding in the preheated oven for 45 minutes, until the surface feels dry and springs back when lightly touched. Serve warm with light cream for pouring, if liked.

baked brioche pudding
with blackberries

This is an impressive dessert for relatively little work. The sweet and buttery brioche works well with the tangy blackberries. Try and buy very sweet blackberries for this, as they will be softer and juicier. The dark purple juices should bleed into the pudding to create a pretty, marbled effect.

4 brioche rolls or ½ a 14-oz. brioche loaf

3 tablespoons butter, softened

2 cups fresh blackberries

3 eggs

⅓ cup heavy cream

1½ cups full-fat milk

⅓ cup sugar

2 tablespoons raw sugar

vanilla ice cream, to serve

a medium baking dish

Serves 6

Slice the brioche to give you 6–8 thin slices. Lightly butter the slices on one side and arrange them in the bottom of the baking dish, overlapping them slightly. Put half the blackberries on top. Repeat with the remaining brioche slices and blackberries. Put the cream, eggs, milk, and sugar in a bowl and beat to combine. Pour the mixture over the brioche in the baking dish. Cover with foil and let sit for 30 minutes to allow the brioche to absorb the liquid.

Preheat the oven to 350°F. Sprinkle the raw sugar over the top of the pudding and bake in the preheated oven for 40–45 minutes, until the top of the pudding is golden brown. Serve warm with vanilla ice cream

fig and honey croissant pudding

Fresh figs have a sweet, honey-nectar flavor. Once picked, they ripen very quickly and late-season figs are perfect cooked in desserts or enjoyed with cheese.

2 croissants, preferably stale, each torn into 6 pieces

6 fresh figs, halved

¼ cup clear honey

3 eggs

1 cup full-fat milk

1 cup light cream

¼ cup sugar

heavy cream, to serve

a medium ovenproof dish, lightly buttered

Serves 4

Preheat the oven to 350°F.

Put the croissant pieces in the bottom of the prepared baking dish. Arrange the fig halves in between the croissant pieces and drizzle the honey over the top.

Combine the eggs, milk, cream, and sugar in a bowl and pour into the dish. Let stand for about 20 minutes so that the croissants can absorb some of the custard. Bake in the preheated oven for 50 minutes, until the top of the pudding is a dark golden brown.

Let cool a little before cutting into slices and serving with heavy cream on the side.

Variation: When figs aren't in season, you can lightly spread each piece of croissant with some good-quality fig jelly before putting into the dish. Leave out the honey and add ⅓ cup slivered almonds to the egg mixture instead.

poached pear tiramisù

Tiramisù is probably one of the best-loved sweets in the world. It has all the essential elements of a perfect dessert—alcohol, creamy custard, and cocoa. Pears work particularly well with anything creamy and cheesy so mascarpone makes an ideal partner. Choose your pears carefully. Soft, sweet varieties such as Packham, do not poach well and will end up as an overly sweet mush. Bosc are good but any fresh firm brown variety will work in this recipe.

6–8 sponge fingers (Italian savoiardi cookies)

1 cup Marsala or brandy

½ cup plus 1 tablespoon sugar

2 firm brown pears (such as Bosc), peeled, cored, and cut into eighths

2 egg whites

4 egg yolks

1 cup mascarpone cheese

unsweetened cocoa powder, to dust

4 individual serving dishes

Serves 4

Line the bottom of each serving dish with sponge fingers, breaking them in order to fit them in.

Put the Marsala or brandy, half of the sugar and ½ cup water in a nonstick skillet and cook over high heat until the mixture reaches a boil, stirring until the sugar has dissolved. Add the pears and cook at a gentle simmer for 20 minutes, turning them often until they are soft and glossy and there is about half of the liquid remaining.

Lay the pears on top of the sponge fingers and pour over the poaching liquid. Using electric beaters, beat the egg whites until firm peaks form. Beat the egg yolks with the remaining sugar for about 5 minutes, until they are pale in color and doubled in size, then beat in the mascarpone.

Using a large metal spoon, fold the egg whites into the yolk and sugar mixture and spoon over the pears. Cover each dish with plastic wrap and refrigerate until ready to serve. Dust each one with a little cocoa powder just before serving.

Note This dessert contains raw eggs, see note on page 4.

baked apples
with dates and sticky toffee sauce

This has the same sticky toffee sauce that is traditionally used in the English baked pudding, but in this recipe the tartness and spiciness of the apples cuts through the sweet, buttery toffee sauce. Sticky toffee sauce is very versatile and can be served with ice cream or spooned over other baked fruit, such as bananas, pears, peaches, or apricots. The apples can be prepared in the morning and popped into the oven as soon as you get home.

sticky toffee sauce

5 tablespoons unsalted butter

⅓ cup soft dark brown sugar

5 tablespoons heavy cream

stuffed apples

⅓ cup dried dates, roughly chopped

1 oz. stem ginger in syrup, drained and finely chopped

2 tablespoon walnuts or pecans, chopped

4 large cooking apples, such as Granny Smith or Courtland, cored

light cream or vanilla ice cream, to serve

a medium baking dish or roasting pan

Serves 4

Preheat the oven to 300°F.

To make the sticky toffee sauce, put the butter, sugar, and cream in a saucepan and set over low heat until melted. Bring to a boil and cook for 1 minute. Remove from the heat and set aside.

Mix together the dates, ginger, and nuts. Stuff half this mixture into the cored apples and stir the remainder into the toffee sauce.

Arrange the stuffed apples in an ovenproof dish or roasting pan so that they fit tightly. Pour the toffee sauce over the apples and cover the entire dish or pan with foil.

Bake in the preheated oven for 25–30 minutes, basting the apples with the sauce occasionally. Remove the dish from the oven and let the apples cool for a few minutes. Serve whilst still warm, with light cream for pouring or vanilla ice cream, as preferred.

freshly squeezed juice of 1 lemon
(about 3 tablespoons)

9 just-ripe, small Conference pears

3 tablespoons butter, softened

3 tablespoons fragrant honey

⅔ cup Premières Côtes de Bordeaux or
late-harvested Sauvignon or Semillon

⅓ cup pine nuts

2 teaspoon raw sugar

¾ cup heavy cream

2 teaspoons vanilla sugar or ½ teaspoon real
vanilla extract and 2 teaspoons sugar

*a large roasting pan or ovenproof dish (big
enough to take the pears in a single layer),
well buttered*

Serves 6

Preheat the oven to 375°F.

Strain the lemon juice into a small bowl.
Cut each pear in half, peel it, and cut away
the core. Dip it in the lemon juice to stop it
discoloring. Place it cut-side upwards in the
roasting pan. Arrange the pears so that they
fit snugly in one layer. Put a knob of butter
in the center of each half. Drizzle the pears
with the honey and pour over the leftover
lemon juice and the wine.

Bake in the preheated oven for 50–60
minutes, turning the pears halfway through.
If the pears produce a lot of juice turn the
heat up to 400°F to concentrate the juices
and form a syrup. Remove from the oven
and let cool for about 20 minutes.

Meanwhile, toast the pine nuts lightly in
a dry skillet, shaking them occasionally
until they start to brown. Sprinkle over the
sugar and continue to cook until the sugar
melts and caramelizes. Sweeten the cream
with the vanilla sugar and heat until warm.
Arrange 3 pear halves on each plate,
drizzle over about 1 tablespoon of warm
cream and scatter over the pine nuts.
Serve immediately.

roast pears
with sweet wine, honey, and pine nuts

Roasting pears in wine transforms them from everyday fruit into a light but
luxurious dessert. The trick is to use an inexpensive wine for cooking and
a better wine of the same type to serve with it.

rhubarb clafoutis

In summer, many French bistro menus feature clafoutis, a custard-like batter baked with whole cherries. It is one of the finest French desserts, and a snip to make. The only drawback is that the cherry season is a short one, and it is a shame to limit clafoutis making to just one part of the year. In fall and winter plums, pears, and apples work well, but rhubarb is fantastic. Almost better than the original.

1 lb. fresh rhubarb, cut into thick slices

¾ cup full-fat milk

¾ cup heavy cream

3 eggs

¾ cup sugar

¼ teaspoon ground cinnamon

a pinch of salt

1 vanilla bean

⅛ cup all-purpose flour

light cream, to serve (optional)

a large baking dish, buttered and sprinkled with sugar

Serves 6

Preheat the oven to 400°F.

Bring a saucepan of water to a boil, add the rhubarb and cook for 2 minutes, just to blanch. Drain and set aside.

Put the milk, cream, eggs, sugar, cinnamon, and salt in a bowl and mix well. Split the vanilla bean lengthwise and scrape the seeds into the mixture. Add the flour and whisk well. Arrange the rhubarb pieces in the prepared baking dish. Pour the batter over the top and bake in the preheated oven for 40–45 minutes, until puffed and golden. Serve warm with cream, if liked.

coffee and chestnut roulade

Here coffee cream, enriched with luscious chestnut purée and rolled up inside a light, golden sponge cake, then drizzled with a bitter-sweet mocha sauce, makes a wickedly indulgent special occasion dessert.

4 eggs

½ cup sugar, plus extra to sprinkle

¾ cup self-rising flour

¼ cup sweetened chestnut purée

coffee cream

3 egg yolks

2 tablespoons sugar

3 tablespoons all-purpose flour

½ cup light cream

⅔ cup full-fat milk

2½ teaspoons instant coffee granules dissolved in 1 tablespoon boiling water

mocha sauce

3 oz. good quality dark bittersweet chocolate (minimum 70% cocoa solids)

⅓ cup freshly brewed espresso coffee

¾ cup heavy cream

a 13 x 9-inch jelly roll pan, greased and lined with baking parchment

Serves 6

To make the coffee cream, whisk together the egg yolks, sugar, and flour until pale and creamy. Heat the cream and milk in a pan until hot but not boiling, then gradually whisk into the egg mixture. Return to the pan and heat very gently for 5–10 minutes, stirring until thick. Stir in the instant coffee, then pour into a bowl, press plastic wrap on to the surface and leave to cool. Chill.

To make the mocha sauce, break the chocolate into pieces and put it in a pan with the espresso and cream. Heat gently,

stirring, until smooth and creamy. Pour into a pitcher and set aside to cool until needed.

Preheat the oven to 425°F.

Put the eggs and sugar in a bowl and whisk for about 10 minutes until thick and pale and the whisk leaves a trail when lifted. Sift over about one-third of the flour and fold in, then repeat with the remaining thirds of flour. Pour into the prepared jelly roll pan, tapping the edges so that it spreads out evenly, and bake for about 10 minutes, or until golden.

Lay a clean kitchen towel on the work surface, sprinkle with sugar and turn the cake out onto it. Carefully peel off the paper, then roll the sponge up like a jelly roll. Leave to cool completely.

To assemble, carefully unroll the cake and spread the coffee cream over the surface, leaving a little space around the edges. Spoon over the chestnut purée, then carefully re-roll using the kitchen towel to support the cake. Serve in slices, drizzled with the mocha sauce.

caramel custard

These are neither too sweet, nor too heavy; the perfect ending to any meal. Either serve them in their ramekins or inverted onto a plate in a pool of sauce.

3 cups full-fat milk

1 vanilla bean

¾ cup plus 2 tablespoons sugar

5 eggs

a pinch of salt

8 ramekin dishes

a roasting pan large enough to hold the ramekins

Serves 8

Put the milk in a large saucepan and set over medium heat. Split the vanilla bean lengthwise and scrape the seeds directly into the milk. Add the vanilla bean to the pan and bring to a boil. Remove from the heat, cover, and let stand.

To make the caramel, put ½ cup of the sugar, the salt, and ¼ cup water in a small heavy-based saucepan. Heat until the sugar turns a deep caramel color, then remove from the heat. When it stops sizzling, pour into the ramekins. Set the ramekins in the roasting pan and add enough boiling water to come half-way up the sides. Set aside.

Preheat the oven to 350°F.

Add the remaining sugar and the salt to the saucepan of warm milk and stir until dissolved. Remove the vanilla bean. Crack the eggs into another bowl and whisk until smooth. Pour the warm milk into the eggs and stir well. Ladle into the ramekins.

Carefully transfer the roasting pan with the ramekins to the preheated oven and bake until the custard is set and a knife inserted into the center comes out clean, about 20–25 minutes. Serve at room temperature.

chocolate and cabernet pots

Combining chocolate with a strong red wine might sound like an unlikely idea, but when you consider the wine's red berry flavors it makes more sense. The ideal wine to use is one that is ripe and fruity but not too oaky, such as a Cabernet.

¾ cup medium-bodied fruity red wine, such as Cabernet Sauvignon

2 tablespoons sugar

7 oz. good quality dark bittersweet chocolate (minimum 70% cocoa solids)

1¼ cups light cream

1 egg

a pinch of ground cinnamon

unsweetened cocoa powder, to dust

confectioners' sugar (optional)

6 or 8 small pots, ramekins or espresso coffee cups, each about ½ cup capacity

Serves 6–8

Put the wine and sugar in a heavy-based saucepan and heat gently until the sugar has dissolved. Increase the heat very slightly and simmer gently for about 20–25 minutes, until the wine has reduced by two-thirds to about 4 tablespoons.

Meanwhile, break the chocolate into pieces, and put them in a blender. Whizz briefly to break them into smaller pieces.

Put the cream in a saucepan and heat until almost at a boil. Pour the hot cream over the chocolate in the blender, then add the hot, sweetened wine. Leave for a few seconds so the chocolate melts. Whizz briefly until the mixture is smooth. Add the egg and cinnamon and whizz again briefly.

Pour the mixture into the ramekins or cups, then chill in the refrigerator for 3–4 hours. Remove the chocolate pots from the refrigerator 20 minutes before serving. To serve, dust each one with a thin layer of cocoa powder then sprinkle with a little sifted confectioners' sugar, if using.

Note This dessert contains raw egg, see note on page 4.

chocolate chile truffles

Pass round these surprisingly warm and mysterious truffles instead of a dessert.

10 oz. good quality dark bittersweet chocolate (minimum 70% cocoa solids)

4 tablespoons unsalted butter, cut into cubes

1¼ cups heavy cream

¼ teaspoon hot chili powder

2 tablespoons chili vodka

unsweetened cocoa powder, to dust

Candied Bird's Eye Chiles, to garnish (optional)

a shallow roasting pan

Makes about 20

Put the chocolate, butter, cream, and chili powder in a bowl set over a saucepan of simmering water. Heat until melted—the mixture should be just tepid. Stir occasionally. Stir in the vodka.

Pour into a shallow pan and refrigerate until firm. Scoop out teaspoonfuls of mixture, roll into rough balls and chill. Sift the cocoa powder onto a plate. Carefully roll each ball in the cocoa. Chill until set. Store in an airtight container in the refrigerator for up to 2 weeks. Serve in little espresso cups with a Candied Bird's Eye Chile, if liked.

Note Candied Bird's Eye Chiles
These are easy to make and are always quite a talking point served with the truffles. Do remember, they are very hot! Dissolve 1¼ cups sugar in 1¼ cups water in a medium saucepan. Bring to a boil for 1 minute. Add 2 oz. whole bird's eye chiles and bring to a boil. Simmer for 15 minutes, then turn off the heat and leave to soak in the syrup for 24 hours. Lift out of the syrup with a fork, drain well, and arrange on nonstick baking parchment. Use immediately or roll in sugar to coat and let dry at room temperature for 24 hours. Store in layers in an airtight box for up to 1 month.

drinks

egg nog

Once you've tasted this deliciously light, foamy punch you'll want to make it every year. This recipe is adapted from a recipe in top American bartender Dale Degroff's 'The Craft of the Cocktail'.

3 very fresh large eggs

⅓ cup superfine sugar

6 tablespoons bourbon

6 tablespoons spiced rum

2⅓ cups full-fat milk

1 cup plus 2 tablespoons whipping cream

freshly grated nutmeg, to taste

Makes 6–8 cups

Separate the egg yolks carefully from the whites and put them in separate large bowls. Beat the egg yolks with an electric hand-held whisk, gradually adding ¼ cup of the sugar, until they turn light in color and moussey in texture. Beat in the bourbon and spiced rum, then stir in the milk and cream.

Clean and dry your whisk thoroughly then whisk the egg whites until beginning to stiffen. Add the remaining sugar to the whites and whisk until they form a soft peak. Fold the whites into the egg nog and grate over a little nutmeg. Ladle out the egg nog into small glasses or cups.

Note This drink contains raw eggs, see note on page 4.

mulled cider

This makes a deliciously fruity and lighter alternative to mulled wine.

2 cups hard apple cider

½ cup Calvados (French apple brandy) or brandy

3 cups soft apple cider or apple juice

⅓ cup soft brown sugar

a thinly pared strip of lemon peel

2 cinnamon sticks

8 cloves

6 even-size slices of dried apple, halved, to garnish

Makes 10–12 cups

Put the hard cider, Calvados, and soft cider in a large saucepan. Add the sugar, lemon peel, cinnamon sticks, and cloves and heat very gently until the sugar has dissolved. Heat until almost boiling, then turn off the heat, add the apple slices and leave the pan to sit for 30 minutes to allow the flavors to infuse. Gently reheat the punch, taking care not to let it reach a boil. Ladle into cups or heatproof glasses to serve, adding a slice of dried apple to each serving.

orange-mulled wine

If you've never made mulled wine yourself, you should try. It couldn't be simpler and tastes infinitely better than the ready-mixed versions. The only thing you have to be careful about is that the wine doesn't reach a boil.

2 x 750-ml bottles medium-bodied fruity red wine

1 orange studded with cloves, plus a few orange slices to serve

thinly pared peel of ½ a lemon

2 cinnamon sticks

6 cardamom pods, lightly crushed

a little freshly grated nutmeg or a small pinch of ground nutmeg

½ cup soft brown sugar

6 tablespoons orange-flavored liqueur, such as Cointreau or Grand Marnier, or brandy

Makes 14–16 small cups

Pour the wine into a large saucepan with 2 cups cold water. Add the orange, lemon peel, spices, and sugar and heat gently until almost boiling. Turn down to the lowest possible heat so that the liquid barely trembles and simmer for half an hour. Add the orange-flavored liqueur then reheat gently. Strain into a large, warmed bowl and float a few thin slices of orange on top. Ladle into small cups or heatproof glasses to serve.

glögg

This comforting, heart-warming drink is served in cafés in Denmark and Sweden to cheer up bleak winter days. It has a miraculous effect.

2 x 750-ml bottles medium-bodied fruity red wine

⅔ cup sugar

1–1½ cups raisins and slivered almonds

1 cinnamon stick

4 cloves

8 cardamom pods, lightly crushed

1 inch piece of fresh ginger, lightly smashed

¾ cup schnapps or vodka

½ cup brandy or cognac

a small piece of cheesecloth and some kitchen twine

Serves 8

Pour 1 bottle of red wine into a nonmetal bowl or saucepan. Add the sugar, raisins, and almonds and stir to dissolve the sugar. Put the spices in the cheesecloth, tie with twine, and add to the wine. Leave to infuse for a couple of hours if possible.

Heat the wine until almost at a boil, then cover and leave to infuse for at least 30 minutes. When ready to serve, remove the spice bag and pour in the second bottle of wine, the schnapps, and the brandy. Reheat until almost at a boil and serve in cups or heatproof glasses along with small spoons.

spiced tea

This fragrant tea is particularly reviving after a winter's walk. You can make it as strong or as weak as you prefer. If liked, add a teaspoon of sweetened condensed milk to each cup.

1 cinnamon stick

3 cloves

1 star anise

3–4 cardamom pods, lightly crushed

1 heaping tablespoon Indian leaf tea, such as Darjeeling or Assam

condensed milk, to taste (optional)

Serves 6

Put the cinnamon, cloves, star anise, and cardamom pods in a large saucepan, add 1 quart water and bring to a boil. Reduce the heat, cover, and simmer gently for 5 minutes, then stir in the loose tea. Stir well, cover, and leave to infuse for 5 minutes. Strain into a warmed teapot, and serve as it is, or with a teaspoonful of condensed milk added to each cup, if liked.

mocha maple coffee

Coffee and chocolate make perfect partners as this delicious drink proves. The addition of sweet, maple-flavored cream makes this an indulgent treat and the perfect after-dinner drink.

2 cups freshly-brewed hot coffee

2 shots crème de cacao or chocolate syrup

½ cup whipping cream

1 teaspoon maple syrup

grated dark bittersweet chocolate, to sprinkle

Serves 2

Pour the hot coffee into 2 tall heatproof glasses and add a shot of crème de cacao or chocolate syrup to each one.

Lightly whisk the cream and maple syrup together until the mixture is foaming and thickened slightly. Slowly layer the cream over the surface of the coffee using the back of a teaspoon. Sprinkle with grated chocolate and serve immediately.

really good coffee

Good coffee is simple to make and you don't need special pots or machines— just a heatproof pitcher and a strainer. Hot milk makes all the difference for those who take milk in their coffee; it produces a drink that is velvety and keeps hot. Using freshly ground coffee is important—freeze the bag after opening, then use straight from frozen.

4 tablespoons freshly ground coffee

boiling water

hot milk

Serves 2

Pour some hot water into a heatproof pitcher to warm it up. Empty out and add the appropriate amount of coffee per person. Pour on enough recently boiled water just to cover the coffee grounds. Stir and leave for 1 minute to infuse.

Top up with 1¼ cups just-boiled water per person and stir well. Cover and let brew for 5 minutes. Either strain through a tea strainer into cups or into another warmed pitcher. Add hot (not boiled) milk, if using. The coffee will have a "crema" or creamy foam on top if you have followed all the steps, and will have a full, rich flavor.

pumpkin latte

Perfect for Halloween, this thick, richly spiced latte is flavored with pumpkin. If you can find some canned sweetened pumpkin purée, then use this and omit the sugar in the recipe.

Put the milk, pumpkin, sugar (if using), and cinnamon in a saucepan and heat gently, whisking constantly until the mixture just reaches a boil. Transfer to 3 cups or heatproof glasses and stir in the coffee. Serve topped with lightly whipped cream and a dusting of cinnamon sugar.

1½ cups milk

4 oz. cooked sweet pumpkin, mashed or 4 oz. canned sweetened pumpkin purée

3 tablespoons brown sugar (omit if using canned purée)

¼ teaspoon ground cinnamon

1 cup freshly brewed hot coffee

whipped cream and cinnamon sugar, to serve

Serves 3

egg-nog latte

This warming, festive drink with a hint of coffee makes a lovely alternative to the more traditional egg nog. For a non-alcoholic version, omit the rum.

2 cups milk

1 vanilla bean, split lengthwise

2 very fresh eggs

2–3 tablespoons superfine sugar, to taste

½ teaspoon ground cinnamon

a pinch of freshly grated nutmeg

2 tablespoons dark rum (optional)

1 cup freshly brewed hot coffee

Serves 4

Put the milk and vanilla bean in a saucepan and heat gently until the milk just reaches a boil. Put the eggs, sugar, and spices in a bowl and whisk until light and frothy. Stir in the milk, then return the mixture to the pan. Heat gently for 2–3 minutes, stirring constantly, until the mixture thickens slightly. Remove from the heat and stir in the rum, if using, and coffee. Pour into 4 heatproof glasses and serve immediately.

spiced white chocolate

The hint of Asian spice is lovely here with the white chocolate and makes a satisfying and warming drink that's just perfect for bedtime.

2 cups milk

4 star anise

a pinch of freshly grated nutmeg, plus extra to dust

4 oz. white chocolate, finely grated

Serves 2

Put the milk, star anise, and nutmeg in a saucepan and bring slowly to a boil. Simmer gently for 5 minutes then remove from the heat and stir in the chocolate until melted. Let cool for 5 minutes then pour into 2 cups or heatproof glasses, dust with a little grated nutmeg, and serve.

Variation You could use dark, bittersweet chocolate in this drink.

mulled bloody mary

This is totally delicious and tastes exactly as you'd imagine a warmed version of the classic brunch drink to taste. It is perfect for a winter's morning, especially if you have over-indulged the night before!

1 quart tomato juice

1 lemon

1–2 tablespoons Worcestershire sauce, to taste

3–4 oz. vodka

a pinch of celery salt

sea salt and freshly ground black pepper

Serves 4–6

Put the tomato juice in a saucepan. Cut half the lemon into slices and squeeze the juice from the remaining half into the pan. Add the lemon slices, Worcestershire sauce, and some salt and pepper to taste. Bring slowly to a boil and simmer gently, uncovered, for 10 minutes.

Remove the saucepan from the heat and let cool for about 20 minutes. Stir in the vodka and some celery salt to taste. Pour into tall heatproof glasses to serve.

malted milk

There are several popular brands of malted milk available, but it is easy enough to make your own healthy version of this soothing hot drink.

2 cups milk

3 tablespoons barley malt extract

freshly grated nutmeg, to serve

Serves 2

Put the milk and malt extract in a saucepan and heat gently until it just reaches a boil. Whisk the milk with a balloon whisk until frothy then pour it into 2 cups. Grate over a little nutmeg and serve.

honey baba

This is a delicately spiced milk drink infused with a hint of honey. You can always add a little shot of rum to this for a grown-up version.

2 cups milk

2 cinnamon sticks, lightly crushed

2 teaspoons runny honey

cinnamon sugar, to dust

Serves 2

Put the milk and cinnamon sticks in a saucepan and heat gently until the milk just reaches a boiling. Remove from the heat and strain. Add 1 teaspoon honey to each of 2 cups or heat-proof glasses and pour in the cinnamon-infused milk. Dust with a little cinnamon sugar and serve immediately.

hot rum and cider punch

This is a lovely fall drink with slices of apple infused with the flavors of the season—cider, rum, and spices. It makes a great punch for a Halloween party. For a family–friendly, non-alcoholic version, replace the hard cider with soft cider or apple juice and omit the rum.

1 x 500-ml bottle hard cider

2 slices lemon

1 apple, cored and thinly sliced

1 cinnamon stick, crushed

3 cloves

2 tablespoons soft light brown sugar

3 oz. dark rum

Serves 4–6

Put all of the ingredients in a large saucepan and heat gently until the liquid just reaches a boil. Reduce the heat and simmer very gently for about 10 minutes. Remove from the heat and let infuse for 10 minutes. Ladle into cups or heat-proof glasses to serve.

hot buttered rum

This is a simple mulled rum drink with the addition of butter to give it some extra richness. It's perfect for a chilly winter evening.

2 shots dark rum

4 cloves

2 lemon slices

2 teaspoons superfine sugar

1 cup just-boiled water

2 tablespoons unsalted butter

2 cinnamon sticks

Serves 2

Put the rum into 2 heatproof glasses and add the cloves, lemon slices, and sugar. Top up with boiling water and add the butter. Put a cinnamon stick in each glass and use to stir the butter as it melts. Serve immediately.

Christmas milk

This drink has all the flavors of the holiday season in a cup. The star decoration on top is fun, but optional, the drink tastes great either way!

1 quart milk

4 tablespoons raisins

2 tablespoons chopped candied ginger

4 teaspoons clear honey

½ an orange, sliced

¼ cup whipping cream, whipped

cinnamon sugar, to dust

a piece of thin white card and a star-shaped cookie cutter, about 2-inches diameter (optional)

Serves 4–6

Using the cookie cutter as a template, carefully draw a star on the card. Use scissors to cut out the star shape.

Put the milk, raisins, ginger, honey, and orange slices in a saucepan. Heat gently until the liquid just reaches a boil. Divide between 4–6 cups. Spoon the whipped cream over the drinks. Hold the stencil over each drink, making sure that the the star shape is in the center. Lightly dust with cinnamon sugar and remove the stencil to leave a star decoration on top. Repeat with all the drinks and serve immediately.

saffron milk

This drink is aromatic and exotic. The saffron, with its earthy flavor and striking color, is pretty as well as delicious. The condensed milk does make this drink very sweet so, if you prefer, reduce the amount used.

2 cups milk

¼ cup sweetened condensed milk

¼ teaspoon saffron threads, plus extra to serve

3 green cardamom pods, lightly crushed

Serves 2

Put the milk, condensed milk, saffron, and cardamom pods in a saucepan and heat gently, stirring constantly, until the mixture just reaches boiling point. Remove from the heat and let infuse for 5 minutes. Strain the milk into 2 heatproof glasses, sprinkle with a few saffron threads and serve immediately.

Mexican chocolate
with vanilla cream

Mexico is where the world's love affair with chocolate began. It was the Aztecs who first used the cacao bean to make a drink, adding vanilla and spicy chiles but it was the Spanish conquistadors who added sugar and cinnamon and created the hot chocolate we enjoy today. A perfect winter warmer.

4 oz. dark bittersweet chocolate (at least 70% cocoa solids), broken into small pieces

6 cups milk

4 tablespoons sugar

2 teaspoons ground cinnamon

cinnamon sticks, to serve (optional)

vanilla whipped cream

1 cup whipping cream

1 vanilla bean*

Serves 6

To make the vanilla whipped cream, put the cream into a bowl and whisk with an electric beater until light and fluffy, with soft peaks. Split the vanilla bean lengthwise and carefully scrape out all the seeds. Gently fold them into the cream.

To make the Mexican chocolate, put the chocolate pieces in a heatproof bowl and set it over a saucepan of gently simmering water to melt—don't let the bottom of the bowl touch the water or the chocolate will be spoiled.

Pour the milk into a large saucepan and stir in the sugar and cinnamon. Heat until gently simmering but do not let it come to a boil. Whisk a ladleful of the milk into the melted chocolate then pour the mixture back into the saucepan, whisking until smooth. Ladle into 6 mugs. Top each with a generous spoonful of vanilla whipped cream and serve hot with a cinnamon stick stirrer, if using.

*Note Don't throw away the split vanilla bean after use. Put it into a storage jar and cover with sugar to make vanilla sugar that can be used in drinks or for baking.

bellini

This truly indulgent cocktail makes a delicious treat for Christmas Day brunch. Although there are many variations on this recipe, there is one golden rule for the perfect Bellini—always use fresh, ripe peaches to make the juice.

½ a fresh peach, skinned and pitted

½ oz. crème de pêche

a dash of peach bitters (optional)

champagne, to top up

a peach ball, to garnish

Serves 1

Purée the peach flesh in a blender and spoon it into a champagne flute. Pour in the crème de pêche and the bitters, if using, then top up with champagne, stirring carefully and continuously. Garnish with a peach ball (made using a melon baller) and serve immediately.

Campari fizz

This decadent aperitif combines the herby, bitter taste of Campari and the sweetness of sparkling wine with mouthwatering results.

1 oz. Campari

½ teaspoon sugar

chilled sparkling wine, to top up

Serves 1

Pour the Campari into a champagne flute and sweeten with the sugar. Top with chilled sparkling wine and serve immediately.

mimosa

A simple yet effective pairing of champagne and freshly squeezed orange juice, perfect served at any celebratory brunch.

½ glass champagne

freshly squeezed orange juice, to top up

Serves 1

Half-fill a champagne flute with champagne. Top with orange juice, stir gently, and serve.

Turkish chocolate

This elegant martini-style cocktail makes a delightful tipple. To decorate the glass, wipe the rim with lemon juice, or dip into egg white, then dip into the cocoa powder.

2 oz. vodka

2 teaspoons white crème de cacao

2 dashes of rose water

unsweetened cocoa powder, for the glass

Serves 1

Add all the ingredients to a shaker filled with ice. Shake the mixture and strain into a chilled martini glass rimmed with cocoa powder, then serve.

champagne cocktail

This classic cocktail has truly stood the test of time, being as popular now as when it was sipped by stars of the silver screen in the 1940s. With a shot of brandy for an extra kick, it is the perfect drink for a festive celebration.

1 white sugar cube

2 dashes of Angostura bitters

1 oz. brandy

dry champagne, to top up

Serves 1

Place the sugar cube in a champagne flute and moisten with the Angostura bitters. Add the brandy and stir, then gently top with the champagne and serve.

brandy alexander

The Brandy Alexander is the perfect after-dinner cocktail—luscious, seductive, and great for chocolate lovers. It is important to get the proportions just right so that the brandy stands out as the main flavor.

2 oz. brandy

½ oz. crème de cacao

½ oz. heavy cream

freshly grated nutmeg, to dust

Serves 1

Add all the ingredients to a cocktail shaker filled with ice. Shake and strain into a chilled martini glass. Dust with grated nutmeg and serve.

black velvet

This one of the most tempting and drinkable cocktails. Pour gently into the glass to allow for the unpredictable nature of both the Guinness and the champagne.

½ a glass Guinness

champagne, to top up

Serves 1

Half-fill a champagne flute with Guinness, gently top with champagne and serve.

black russian

The Black Russian is a classic that has been around for many years. The sweet coffee flavor of the Kahlúa is sharpened by the vodka to create this stylish after-dinner cocktail.

2 oz. vodka

1 oz. Kahlúa

a maraschino cherry, to garnish

Serves 1

Add the vodka and Kahlúa to a cocktail shaker filled with ice. Shake and strain into a rocks glass filled with ice, garnish with a cherry and serve.

white russian

This twist on the Black Russian has the addition of cream. It's an indulgent treat that makes the perfect nightcap.

2 oz. vodka

1 oz. Kahlúa

1 oz. light cream

a maraschino cherry, to garnish

Serves 1

Add the vodka and Kahlúa to a cocktail shaker filled with ice. Shake and strain into a rocks glass filled with ice, then gently layer on the cream over the back of a teaspoon. Garnish with a cherry and serve.

vodka espresso

This elegant little cocktail makes the perfect after dinner pick-me-up as it combines freshly made espresso coffee with a dash of vodka.

2 oz. vodka

1 shot freshly made strong espresso coffee

a dash of sugar syrup

3 coffee beans, to garnish (optional)

Serves 1

Pour the espresso coffee into a cocktail shaker. Add a generous measure of vodka and sugar syrup to taste. Shake the mixture up sharply and strain into an old fashioned glass filled with ice. The vigorous shaking should have created a foamy "crema" which will sit on top on the drink. Garnish with three coffee beans, if liked, and serve immediately.

vodka cranberry floaters

This pretty party drink tastes and looks heavenly. The blueberries add a colorful touch to this vodka classic.

1 oz. chilled vodka

½ cup cranberry juice

ice cubes, to serve

blueberries, to decorate

Serves 1

Put the vodka in a tall glass and add the cranberry juice. Mix well. Add a few blueberries, then some ice cubes. Serve immediately.

brown cow

This cocktail is perfect for serving to a party crowd as it only requires two ingredients and minimal preparation.

½ bottle Kahlúa (12 oz.)

1 quart milk

ice cubes

Serves 8

Put all the ingredients in a large pitcher and mix. Alternatively, put the Kahlúa in ice-filled glasses and top up with milk.

New Orleans sazarac

These is a great drink for those who enjoy a warming whisky. It can be topped with water or soda to make a thirst quencher but to fully enjoy the flavors it should be drunk undiluted. If you enjoy the aniseed flavor of Pernod, try adding it to the drink rather than rinsing the glass with it.

2 oz. bourbon

1 oz. Pernod

1 sugar cube

Angostura bitters

Serves 1

Rinse an old-fashioned glass with Pernod and discard the Pernod. Put the sugar in the glass, saturate with Angostura bitters, then add ice cubes and the bourbon and serve.

hot toddy

This warming blend of spices and sweet honey is the perfect comforter and will soothe any aches and snuffles that your winter cold may have inflicted upon you. It's also a great life-saver for cold afternoons spent outside watching sport. Next time you have need to pack a Thermos of coffee, think again—mix up a batch of Hot Toddies, and see how popular you are!

5 whole cloves

2 lemon slices

2 oz. whisky

1 oz. freshly squeezed lemon juice

2 teaspoons honey

3 oz. hot water

1 cinnamon stick (optional)

Serves 1

Skewer the cloves into the lemon slices and put them in a heat-proof glass. Pour in the whisky and lemon juice. Add the honey and top up with the water. Stir well and garnish with the cinnamon stick, if using, to serve.

conversion charts

Weights and measures have been rounded up
or down slightly to make measuring easier.

Volume equivalents:

American	Metric	Imperial
1 teaspoon	5 ml	
1 tablespoon	15 ml	
¼ cup	60 ml	2 fl.oz.
⅓ cup	75 ml	2½ fl.oz.
½ cup	125 ml	4 fl.oz.
⅔ cup	150 ml	5 fl.oz. (¼ pint)
¾ cup	175 ml	6 fl.oz.
1 cup	250 ml	8 fl.oz.

1 stick butter = 8 tablespoons = 125 g

Weight equivalents:		Measurements:	
Imperial	Metric	Inches	cm
1 oz.	25 g	¼ inch	5 mm
2 oz.	50 g	½ inch	1 cm
3 oz.	75 g	¾ inch	1.5 cm
4 oz.	125 g	1 inch	2.5 cm
5 oz.	150 g	2 inches	5 cm
6 oz.	175 g	3 inches	7 cm
7 oz.	200 g	4 inches	10 cm
8 oz. (½ lb.)	250 g	5 inches	12 cm
9 oz.	275 g	6 inches	15 cm
10 oz.	300 g	7 inches	18 cm
11 oz.	325 g	8 inches	20 cm
12 oz.	375 g	9 inches	23 cm
13 oz.	400 g	10 inches	25 cm
14 oz.	425 g	11 inches	28 cm
15 oz.	475 g	12 inches	30 cm
16 oz. (1 lb.)	500 g		
2 lbs.	1 kg		

Oven temperatures:

110°C	(225°F)	Gas ¼
120°C	(250°F)	Gas ½
140°C	(275°F)	Gas 1
150°C	(300°F)	Gas 2
160°C	(325°F)	Gas 3
180°C	(350°F)	Gas 4
190°C	(375°F)	Gas 5
200°C	(400°F)	Gas 6
220°C	(425°F)	Gas 7
230°C	(450°F)	Gas 8
240°C	(475°F)	Gas 9

recipe credits

GHILLIE BASAN

chickpea salad with onions and paprika
classic lamb tagine with almonds, prunes, and apricots
lamb, chickpea, and lentil soup with cumin
lamb tagine with chestnuts, saffron, and pomegranate seeds
plain, buttery couscous
spicy carrot and chickpea tagine with turmeric and cilantro
spicy potato omelet

FIONA BECKETT

boeuf bourguignon
chestnut and puy lentil soup with celeriac cream
chocolate and cabernet pots
coq au vin
cranberry and cherry Florentines
crunchy roast potatoes
egg nog
ginger and cinnamon thins
Italian-style roast pork with white wine, garlic, and fennel
Languedoc beef stew with red wine, herbs, and olives
mulled cider
orange-mulled wine
pomme purée
pot roast brisket with red wine
pumpkin soup with honey and sage
roast beef tenderloin with soy and butter sauce
roast monkfish with pancetta, rosemary, and red wine gravy
roast pears with sweet wine, honey, and pine nuts
roast pumpkin and pecan pie
smoked duck, mandarin, and pecan salad with pinot noir dressing

SUSANNAH BLAKE

coffee and chestnut roulade
coffee and walnut cake
coffee, macadamia, and white choc chunk cookies
mini croque-monsieurs
Parmesan and bacon pancakes with chive butter
smoked trout rarebit
stem ginger cookies
sticky marzipan and cherry loaf
toasted teacakes

MAXINE CLARK

a big pot of cassoulet
apple, prune, and Armagnac phyllo crumble
chocolate chile truffles
classic blackberry and apple crumble
dukkah
fluffy potato pancakes with smoked salmon
glögg
goat cheese, leek, and walnut tart
gooseberry and ginger wine crumble
herb- and nut-crusted salmon fillets
lemony apple crumble tart
Mexican pork and beans in red chile sauce
mulled winter fruit crumble
mushroom, cognac, and cream risotto
oven-roasted spiced nuts
perfect mashed potatoes
perfect roast beef with herbed Yorkshire puddings
petits pois à la Francaise
plum and hazelnut pandowdy
polenta baked with Italian sausage and cheese
pork loin roasted with rosemary and garlic
pot roast leg of lamb with rosemary and onion sauce
potato and Parmesan tart
real treacle tart with caramelized bananas
really good coffee
smoked salmon and chive soufflé omelet
spiced tea
steak and wild mushroom pies
sticky date flaky tarts with caramel oranges
tomato and eggplant gratin with tomato and chili pesto
vichy carrots with fresh ginger

LINDA COLLISTER

chocolate brandy cake
Christmas mini-muffins
gingerbread mini-muffins
iced star cookies
Swedish saffron cake
triple chocolate brownies

ROSS DOBSON

apple and blueberry tarts
baked brioche pudding with blackberries
baked Granny Smith and blueberry pudding
baked mushrooms with Manchego béchamel
baked spinach mornay
buttermilk mash
carrot and lentil soup
cauliflower and Swiss chard salad
chicken, leek, and tarragon pot pie
creamy cauliflower and Gruyère soup
crispy onion rings with Parmesan aïoli
crispy oven wedges with homemade pesto sauce
dusky apple pie
egg, bacon, and spinach pie
fig and honey croissant pudding
mushroom and thyme ragù with hand-torn pasta
pasta with broccoli, walnuts, and ricotta
pear and ginger crumble cake
poached pear tiramisù
potato and parsnip croquettes
pumpkin and Gorgonzola risotto
red curry of roasted fall vegetables
roast beef rib-eye with winter vegetables and garlic crème
roasted early fall vegetables with chickpeas
roasted pork with apple and fennel puddings
roasted tomato soup with rarebit toasts
sage pork chops with kale colcannon
salad of winter fruit with blue cheese and spinach
sausages with celeriac rösti
slow-cooked Brussels sprouts with pancetta and chestnuts
slow-cooked onion and cider soup with Gruyère toasts
smashed roast new potatoes
smoky hotpot of great northern beans
smoky sausage and bean casserole
spaghetti with butternut squash, sage, and pecorino
spiced cauliflower with red bell peppers and peas
spicy red vegetable soup
Swiss chard, feta cheese, and egg pie
taleggio and potato tortilla with red bell pepper tapenade
trio of vegetable dips with spelt toasts
vegetable ragù with spiced couscous
winter vegetable gratin
winter vegetable tagine with apple and mint

LYDIA FRANCE

snowy pine nut cookies
trio of honey-baked camembert
warm cheese scones with cheddar and pickled pears

LIZ FRANKLIN

chicken, raisin, and chile salad with hazelnut dressing
mushrooms marinated with raisins and apple cider vinegar
pan-fried tuna steaks with warm vincotto-dressed lentils
poulet sauté au vinaigre
roast onion and celeriac ravioli with walnut pesto
roasted butternut squash and pancetta salad with pumpkin oil and spiced dressing
sticky pork fillet with pecorino crust, mustard mash, and balsamic onion

MANISHA GAMBHIR HARKINS

Mexican chocolate with vanilla cream
spiced tomato and lentil salad

TONIA GEORGE

herby sausages on polenta with red onion and red currant gravy
leek and potato soup
monkfish, fennel, and saffron bourride
mushroom soup with Madeira and hazelnuts

parsnip, chorizo, and chestnut soup
potato, bacon, and Savoy cabbage soup
smoked haddock and bean soup
winter-spiced salad with pears, honeyed pecans, and ricotta

KATE HABERSHON

crumpets

CAROLINE MARSON

baked apples with dates and sticky toffee sauce
chunky fish stew with cheese toasts
harissa-spiced chickpeas with halloumi and spinach
individual caramelized pear and cranberry tarts
quick Thai chicken curry
roasted butternut squash risotto

LOUISE PICKFORD

Campari fizz
Christmas milk
egg-nog latte
French fries
honey baba
hot buttered rum
hot rum and cider punch
malted milk
mimosa
mocha maple coffee
mulled bloody mary
pumpkin latte
saffron milk
spiced white chocolate

BEN REED

bellini
black Russian
black velvet
brandy alexander
champagne cocktail
hot toddy
New Orleans sazarac
Turkish chocolate
vodka espresso
white Russian

FIONA SMITH

beef and ale pâté

SONIA STEVENSON

roast turkey with lemon and herb stuffing

FRAN WARDE

baked and glazed ham
beef en croûte with mustard sauce
beet, goat cheese, and pine nut salad with melba toasts
chicken jalfrezi
country chicken
garlic sautéed green beans
mountain eggs
Parmesan and rosemary wafers
roasted pheasant breasts with bacon, shallots, and mushrooms
roasted rack of lamb with a spicy crust
roasted salmon wrapped in prosciutto
vodka cranberry floaters

LAURA WASHBURN

baked plums in puff pastry with crème fraîche
butternut squash with pistou
caramel custard
carrots with cream and herbs
cauliflower gratin
cauliflower with garlic and anchovies
chili with all the trimmings
creamy potato gratin
harissa potatoes
meatballs in spicy red sauce
pear and almond tart
pork in cider with potatoes and apples
Portuguese lamb stew with piri piri
rhubarb clafoutis
roast beets
roast chicken with bay leaves, thyme, and lemon
savoy cabbage with bacon and cream
sweet potatoes with thyme and chile
wilted greens

photography credits

MARTIN BRIGDALE
pages 1, 32, 33r, 34, 58l, 59, 73, 77, 78l, 91, 97b, 104b, 105b, 122, 125, 128 both, 131l, 132r, 135a, 136a, 137l, 137br, 139, 153, 154l

DAVID BRITTAIN
pages 70a, 130

PETER CASSIDY
pages 2, 4l, 8, 10, 11, 16l, 24, 36, 43r, 48, 50a, 61r, 65, 66, 67ac, 76r, 84, 86, 87ac, 89al, 92, 94, 119r, 120 both, 124r, 127, 138, 141bl, 142, 143l, 144, 145b, 146, 147, 150b, 151a, 152, 157al, 157ar, 158 both, 159, 167r

JEAN CAZALS
page 25r

CHRISTOPHER DRAKE
pages 85b (interior designer Carole Oulhen/+ 33 6 80 99 66 16), 109r

RICHARD JUNG
pages 9ar, 9b, 12, 13r, 14, 15, 26, 29, 30, 31a, 38, 39r, 41, 42, 47, 50b, 51, 52, 53 both, 54ar, 54b, 55, 56l, 58ar, 60l, 62, 64r, 70b, 71, 78r, 79, 81r, 83 both, 90, 93, 100, 101ac, 102, 107 main, 108b, 110, 114, 117, 119l, 121, 123a all, 134, 140, 143r, 148, 149, 150a

SANDRA LANE
pages 25al, 43l, 67ar, 95b, 96al, 97l, 98ar, 107 inset, 112al, 124l, 135b, 166al, 166ac, 169b both

TOM LEIGHTON
page 13l

WILLIAM LINGWOOD
pages 23r, 25bl, 35, 40r, 46, 58br, 69, 80, 82, 88b, 99, 101al, 104a, 154r, 155l, 156, 161r, 162 both, 163r, 164, 165 both, 166ar, 167l, 168 both, 169a, 170, 171 both, 173 both

JASON LOWE
page 85a

JAMES MERRELL
endpapers, 16r, 18l, 61l, 88a, 103a, 145a, 151b

DAVID MONTGOMERY
pages 141al

DAVID MUNNS
pages 44, 68a, 75, 105a, 111a, 112ar, 112b, 113, 141r

NOEL MURPHY
pages 9al, 22r, 23l, 57, 74, 81l, 95a, 103b, 106, 155r, 160l, 161l

WILLIAM REAVELL
pages 40l, 118, 126, 129, 131r, 132l, 133

YUKI SUGIURA
pages 17, 18r, 19, 20, 21

DEBI TRELOAR
pages 3, 5, 6, 9ac, 22l, 28, 31b, 33l, 37al, 37ac, 37b, 39l, 45, 60r, 64l, 67al, 67b, 68b, 76bl, 87al, 87ar, 87b, 89bl, 89r, 96bl, 96r, 98al, 98b, 101ar, 101b, 111b, 115, 116 both, 157b, 172

CHRIS TUBBS
pages 4r (Emily Todhunter/www.todhunterearle.com), 37ar, 49, 160r, 163l

JO TYLER
pages 76al, 123b, 136b, 166b

ALAN WILLIAMS
pages 109l, 157ac

ANDREW WOOD
page 108a (Mark Pynn/www.sunvalleyarchitect.com)

POLLY WREFORD
pages 54al, 137ar